Jesus Help Me

An Adventure of Miracles, Music, and Mercy

Judith E. King

Jesus Help Me: An Adventure of Miracles, Music, and Mercy

© 2020 Judith E. King

Published in the United States

judithevelynking@gmail.com

Content Editor: Lorilee Reimer Craker

Editor, Producer: Gerald R. Doctor, geraldrdoctor@gmail.com

Cover Photo: Dr. Stephen King

Cover Design: Deborah K. Allen

To God be the glory!

For Caleb, Parker, Madeline, Campbell, Shelby, Alex, and Lilly, my precious and dearly-loved grandchildren. You all have brought to me such incredible joy as I have watched you grow and enjoyed who God created you to be—each of you with your loving hearts, your incredible giftedness, and your journey with Jesus as Savior.

I want you and your children to know some of your history, and to be encouraged by the stories of God's presence, his miracles, and his faithfulness to Grandpa and me throughout our life of learning and adventure.

Contents

Foreword

I was conducting a pastoral briefing in Toronto, Canada when I first met Dr. Stephen and Judy King. They didn't represent my target audience, and I wasn't the purpose for them being in Toronto, which made our meeting rather providential.

Stephen and Judy had done medical missionary work in Northern Canada with First Nations people who have an animistic worldview and practice Spiritism. They had seen firsthand the reality of the spiritual world, which was radically different from the worldview they would return to when they furthered their education in psychiatry and psychology.

Stephen and Judy were intrigued by this ex-aerospace engineer that acknowledged the reality of the spiritual world, and had actually integrated it into his pastoral ministry. I invited them to take a week off, and come to a conference I was conducting in Calgary, and sit in on some freedom appointments as prayer partners. Upon returning to Grand Rapids they invited me to do a similar conference in their home church, and we have been friends ever since.

We invited both of them to come on the board of Freedom in Christ Ministries, but our board chairman didn't want a husband and wife as members of the same board. So Stephen became a member of the board, and Judy reluctantly deferred, but that didn't mean that Judy wasn't actively participating in the ministry (When has Judy never been active?). She became a community leader like none other in our ministry, and did pioneer research on the effectiveness of discipleship counseling.

I was making my first visit to the funeral home where my father was displayed in an open casket when my cell phone rang. The caller informed me that Stephen had died suddenly of a heart attack. That news hit me harder than the death of my father. Judy and Stephen were special people to me, the kind you wish young people would emulate:

hardworking, responsible, devoted, faithful, caring, and humble.

It is not surprising to anybody who knows Judy that she would grieve greatly, but rise above the circumstances. She not only replaced Stephen on our board, but was chosen by the American staff to represent them (North American and the Caribbean) on the International Board of Freedom in Christ Ministries. I am glad that Judy has chosen to write this memoir of their exemplary life. What a legacy!

Dr. Neil T. Anderson, Founder and President Emeritus of Freedom in Christ Ministries

Preface

"A pleasure is only fully grown when it is remembered." – C.S. Lewis

"It's time to tell your story." – A repetitive echo in my mind.

Tell them the story about when Grandpa attached the arm to that guy and it grew back," my grandson said, as he and some friends of mine were working on a renovation project at my home.

Over the years, my grandchildren have asked questions about Steve and me and our lives together, especially since Steve is no longer here. Of course, I love to tell those stories, and yes, I guess I repeat them. "Grandma, you've already told me that story," the grands have said.

But hear me out; there's a scientific theory related to those repetitions of mine—supported by recent medical and mental health research. As we remember pleasant memories, those parts of the brain that store memories release positive hormones (endorphins, to be exact). So, of course, I want to release as many happy hormones as possible!

Studies also show that, if you meditate on God's love for 20 minutes each day for 30 days, your prefrontal cortex will proliferate. Our brain has plasticity and is not set in stone as previously believed. How's that for encouragement? Grow your brain![1]

I'll take all of the brain growth I can get. I need that help as some of my 30 billion neurons age and go to sleep!

As I've shared some of our adventures and stories over the years, many people have encouraged me to write these stories down for others in addition to just my grandkids. Yesterday when I arrived for my

---

1 Tim Jenner, *The God-Shaped Brain: How Changing Your View of God Transforms Your Life* (Downers Grove, IL: IVP Books, 2013/2017).

art lesson, this suggestion was confirmed again.

"You should write these down," my art teacher, Margaret, said. "Just a little bit each day." I was admiring the globe of the world in Margaret's sitting room, showing her some of the places we had lived—including north of the 60th parallel in the Canadian Arctic.

I was recounting to her our adventures of flying in our four-seater Cessna 172 down the majestic Mackenzie River to the Arctic Ocean, camping under the wing of our plane. We had dried emergency food tucked away onboard should we need it. And Steve had his guitar.

I got carried away as I told Margaret how we had to make many scary landings on seldom-used, ancient wind-swept grass strips along the Mackenzie River. The most frightening one occurred when we were approaching the Inuvik airport, on the Arctic Ocean, and visibility was zero.

Our radio told us that no more flights had permission to land because of the dangerous conditions. We didn't have enough fuel to turn around, and there was no other place to land. Below us were miles of mushy bog …

Jesus, help me! Jesus, help me! Jesus, help us!

But, I'm getting ahead of myself. You'll have to read on to discover the end of that particular story. You'll also have to read on if you want to know if I really was presented to Queen Elizabeth and her family, by none other than former Canadian Prime Minister Jean Chrétien.

Someone who read the first draft of this book suggested that my main reason for writing this memoir seemed more for myself and less from a motive of altruism for others (especially my grandkids as I originally envisioned). Pondering that, I realized there was some truth to it—up to a point.

I had studied Erik Erikson's eight stages of psychosocial development in graduate school. He notes that those over age 65 are in the stage of *integrity* versus *despair*. As a 75-year-old, I guess I fit that category.

Yes, there has been some despair as I've realized mistakes I've made—mistakes now forgiven by God and by others that I have hurt. I've found that repentance and forgiveness are life-giving ingredients in the garden of integrity.

I suppose as we age—or as my doctor kindly said—"progressively mature" that by God's grace, despair can and does morph into integrity. I've experienced that pleasure, joy, and integrity as I've remembered and luxuriated in the warm, thankful feelings this writing has generated.

Yes, it is true that I want to pass on to my grandchildren and to future generations the stories of God's faithfulness in our lives. I hope you also enjoy my stories.

Ultimately, mine is a story of God's incredible faithfulness, love, and healing, with all of the ups and downs we had, many times falling so short of who God would have us to be. Steve and I were young and had growing pains in our marriage, which our children of course observed. Many times we were living from our fleshly nature and not from the Spirit of God within us.

Life is full of failures: sin, repentance, forgiveness, and healing, all undergirded by God's grace. Of course I wish that I could re-do some of those times, to reduce the angst that my children experienced.

However, we did the best that we knew at the time, both of us coming from very imperfect families, trying to figure out how to be a married couple and loving parents. The amazing thing to me is that God uses very imperfect people to carry out his assignments—and that we definitely were.

Steve and I had made the commitment on June 11, 1966, to choose to love through thick and thin. We had many happy years together and shared a deep, committed love, but things were not always peachy keen. Like every marriage in the history of the world, we had our highs and some very low lows.

We sometimes disappointed and hurt each other, and we had to seek forgiveness and grace. Through it all, we learned how to love each other better. We learned to pray together.

At times, when I was feeling unloved, it infused my lonely heart with warmth to hear my husband pray in my presence, "Lord, show me how to love Judy, and help me." Other times, it was me praying that prayer. The main thing was to cling to the main thing: God was the source of our love.

God was there to help us. He wants to help you succeed too. In his book, *The Mystery of Marriage*, Canadian author Mike Mason explains how in marriage God is preparing us to be the bride of Christ.[2]

I share positive stories in this book. After Steve's death, my therapist, Joe, explained that we have to sort through memories and emotions just like we have to sort through our deceased loved one's clothes: some we'll keep and some we'll discard.

My grandson, Caleb, wanted to keep Grandpa's slippers, his plaid shirts, and his housecoat. (I loved that!) My son, David, kept his father's very tacky green pants/red vest, which he still wears (for 5 minutes) on Christmas like his father did.

Other clothing items, like some memories, were discarded, given away, or sent to a thrift store. The other day one of my friends from my care group showed up in a vest of Steve's which I had given him ... and I loved the memories brought back by seeing the vest.

But that doesn't mean we get to be in denial about the negative memories. Before discarding them, we must relive them in God's presence, choosing to forgive and asking Jesus—Jehovah Rapha, the God who heals—to touch those painful wounded spots. He always will, because that is his character. He is a healer.

This exercise takes a lot of inner work and prayer, but the result is freedom and contentment. (In my counseling practice, I have been a witness countless times as I've seen God heal past hurts and resolve personal conflicts, and of course, I have to say, in my own life as well.)

Let's face it, we come from imperfect families, marry someone from an imperfect family, and make an imperfect family. We all need healing of some sort at some time, and this is an ongoing process throughout life's journey.

After a recent second bout of pulmonary embolisms (blood clots) in both of my lungs, I was thrown into confronting my own mortality. Because of the disappointment and fear I experienced, I started seeing a spiritual director/therapist. She significantly helped me resolve some of my past memories that were still there—even as a woman in her 70s.

Can you imagine that? I've been told that I see life through "rose

---

2 Mike Mason, *The Mystery of Marriage* (Colorado Springs, CO: Multnomah Books, 1985/2005).

colored glasses." Even though I am an optimistic soul, could there be some denial mixed in? Carol gave me a pithy quote: "Denial is the drug of a broken heart." Thankfully our God is the healer of broken hearts—of any dimension!

The Psalmist exhorts us to tell of his wonders to the next generation. He wants us to leave a legacy of God's care, power, and miracles in our lives. He wants us to tell the stories of the glory of God to the next generations and encourage them to grow in faith.

Dear ones, my family, even to multiple generations—or whoever reads this book—may it help you restore, encourage, or initiate the foundations of faith in your life.

> Even when I am old and gray, do not forsake me, O God, till I declare your power to the next generation, Your might to all who are to come.

> Your righteousness reaches to the skies, O God, You who have done great things. Who, O God, is like you? (Psalm 71:18-19).

Introduction

I panicked as I sloshed my way through the puddles, a block-and-a-half away to the bus stop. *"Oh, no, I'm going to miss the bus,"* I thought. My new beige seersucker suit—bought in the hopes that it would look professional—crinkled as greasy mud splattered over me.

I needed to arrive at this interview on time, looking crisp, not crumpled. My mother's friend, an executive at BP Oil, had gone out of his way to get me this interview for the job. I needed the money for college tuition, and jobs like this—as a mere inexperienced student—were hard to come by.

As I hobble-ran towards the bus in my (too-high) heels, waving frantically at the driver, I remembered that today was Tuesday. I *so* looked forward to Tuesdays, especially at 5 p.m.—whether or not I made the job interview. (By the way, I did make it to the BP office on time, and was hired, crumples and all.).

Tuesdays at five in the evening were an exciting part of my week that summer. At that time I would receive a phone call from that special guy, my boyfriend, Steve. He would call me from Ellesmere Island, a frozen locale that lay just 300 miles south of the North Pole in the Northwest Territories of the Canadian Arctic.

Steve and I had been dating for nine months. He travelled north that first summer to earn his tuition for medical school. Since Steve had landed in the arctic—a land of muskox, fossils, and eight-foot snow banks—for a four-month stint, working at a joint US/Canada strategic weather station, it had been challenging to communicate.

No cell phones, internet, computers, or even land lines existed there then. To reach me, Steve had to find someone in the Toronto area who had a ham radio with a phone patch. Ray was that man.

Ray listened to every single word between us, and our entire conversation was punctuated by his interruptions. Each time as the speaker changed he had to say "over" and change his settings before the other one spoke. At the end he would say "over and out" to conclude our conversation.

This particular day, after my interview at BP Oil, I ran breathlessly up the stairs, through the screen door, into my house at just a bit past five o'clock. My mother was already on the phone with Steve.

"Just a minute, here she comes through the door," my mother said, sweetly. She adored Steve already. "Oh, I think I'll stay on the call," she teased.

My mother loved to hear news about Steve. He had written me a volume of poetry in addition to the eight-to-ten-page letters that came my way whenever the mail plane would come and go from his arctic depot. Apparently he wrote something every day, as I did also. It was a great way to stay close.

One day I eagerly ripped open the envelope from Steve and began reading it out loud to my mom. Part way through a poem about our love, there was a spicy part about my "luscious lips." I stopped reading immediately, my face aflame. Nobody wants to discuss one's luscious lips with one's own mother.

Over the next four months, Steve and I exchanged our lives, daily activities, thoughts, and feelings from across the miles as Ray listened in the background.

For me in the summer of 1962, the most important conversation in the whole world took place at the same time every week, on Tuesday at five.

***

As a little girl of four, I experienced a miracle when I first consciously uttered those three words, "Jesus, help me!" It was the beginning of my faith journey.

That night in 1948, I had been consumed with fear. I had overheard the grownups talking and speculating that the Russians might come and bomb our city of Toronto. Soon, we'd have to turn out all the lights and blacken the windows, whatever that meant. Adding to my turmoil was the fact that I could hear my parents fighting over our lack of money to pay basic bills.

"The men will be up the pole turning off the electricity and we'll have no more coal for our furnace!" my mother shouted. "We'll all freeze to death!" I had heard it all before, but that didn't make it less unsettling.

My father had his own lithography business, which brought in an unstable, varying income, to say the least—in fact, many weeks, no income! He was a brilliant inventor, very intelligent but a poor businessman.

I remember that, according to family lore, he had invented the lithographic plate to produce wood veneers. But he had either given away the invention, bartered it, or had it stolen. We will never know for sure.

I did know that I was scared, paralyzed with fear at the Russians and filled with anxiety over the unrest in my own home.

"Jesus, please help me," I cried. "Jesus, help me!" I don't know how I even knew to call out to Jesus, since we were not regular churchgoers and I knew no Christians. But I did. I cried out to him in my distress.

And then I saw Jesus at the foot of my bed, the epitome of love and light and tenderness with arms open to me. "I will never leave you or forsake you," He told me. And then He was gone from my vision but not from my spirit.

Was it a vision? I don't know. I just know that I saw him and was comforted. Filled with peace and a tangible feeling of safety, I fell asleep.

Only in later years did I realize there was no way of knowing that those words Jesus spoke to me were written in the Bible. At that point, I had never even seen a Bible with my own eyes. Well, except for the time that a cemetery plot salesman had showed up at our door, bearing a gift of a white, fake-leather, zippered Bible.

I was so mad that the salesman with the crazy felt hat was not a representative from the TV show *The Millionaire*! I certainly wasn't very impressed with his door prize. My siblings and I had been so sure that the mysterious man who had called us to arrange a visit was going to hand over a check for a million dollars. Oh, what dreamers we were.

It was not to be, but I didn't realize at the time that I was already richer than I knew. Jesus was with me, and He would never leave me or forsake me.

For nearly seven decades that vision of Jesus at the foot of my bed has stayed with me. It is a touchstone for a life of trusting in him to be with me, through it all—through the ups and downs of life, and the anxiety that comes with all of that.

I know now in the deepest part of my soul that God is faithful. When we experience deep sorrow and trials and call on him, He is there. *Jesus, help me!* has been my mantra, the automatic cry of my heart, throughout my life of failures, successes, and everything in between. There is power in the name of Jesus.

Many times I have failed in calling out to him with trust and saying his name, but He has always been there for me. So many times I have failed him, but I've come to understand that his love is unconditional and not dependent on my faith or my performance.

This is a story of two flawed people from two wounded families, who made an imperfect marriage and family but who experienced God's amazing grace and ongoing healing through it all, in spite of ourselves. It's all about God's power, "his strength in our weakness."

We were blessed to see many miracles, not because of us but because of his miraculous interventions. To God be all the glory.

***

My relationship with Steve did not end with those weekly calls on Tuesday at five. We got married and had two great children, David and Deborah. We traveled all over the world and had many adventures. Our life story continued for forty-two years, thirty-nine of them as man and wife.

I'm eager to share some of our stories in this book, for posterity, I guess. It's been a lovely healing experience writing this as I've remembered and reminisced.

But first I must tell you briefly about an ending, and how that ending was really a beginning of a phase in my life of trying to find a "new normal." On July 30, 2005, a day that will forever be etched in every layer of my life, I learned that my husband, Steve, had died.

When David and Jean, our upstairs neighbors at our lake condo, gave me the news that broke my heart and changed my life forever, all I could say was, "Jesus, help me … Jesus, help me … Jesus, help me …" over and over again. I had practiced those three words so often throughout my life that they came spontaneously from the depths of my heart.

Jesus, help me! It had been fifty-seven years since I cried out this prayer as a scared little girl. Only Jesus could hold me up as I was falling. Only Jesus could comfort me in this most painful moment of my life. At that point I didn't know if I could make it. Deep, gut-wrenching grief. I'll say more about that later.

The Lord had responded to me with love when I was a child of four. Now He responded to me again with his presence. It was the saddest and most devastating ending in my life as I knew it, but God was still with me.

Someone once told me that Jeremiah 33:3 is God's telephone number: "Call unto me and I will answer you." God knows your number, and now you know his. He wants us to call on him in every moment, both miraculous and mundane, in times of fear, stress, disappointment, and sorrow.

Will you join me on this journey of my life? I hope you will be inspired. As many of you know, I love to tell the stories. This book is filled with these stories and narratives of the miracles, grace, and glory of God, of which I have been an honored witness.

Also, my prayer for you, my family and for generations of families yet to come, is that you will be challenged and encouraged to follow Jesus with all your heart. That He will fill you with the Holy Spirit as He promised, and that you would experience the excitement and the adventure of living a life dedicated to the God of this universe, who is omnipotent, omnipresent, and omniscient.

I bless you in the name of the Father, the Son—our Lord Jesus Christ—and the Holy Spirit, to live your life abundantly.

Judith E. King May, 2020

Chapter 1

Born to Celebrate Life

I will never leave you or forsake you (Hebrews 13:5).

My first conscious memory is of being rescued from drowning by my older sister, Joyce, when I was three. At our summer cottage, I had wandered down to the edge of the boat dock and had fallen in.

I remember bobbing up and down, looking at the lines in the sand and thinking they were telephone poles. I'm thankful for God's protection, since now I'm still alive. Thank you, God. And thank you, Joyce.

This seems to be the pattern of my life: I get in over my head, I call upon God, He rescues me, and I rejoice and give him the glory.

***

The first baby born in 1944 in Toronto, Ontario, wasn't me. But I was a close second.

It was New Year's Eve, 1943, and my mother was preparing for a party at our home on Wanless Street. She had finished cooking her amazing party food and was polishing the floor for her guests when I interrupted. I've always liked a party and I guess I didn't want to miss that one!

When her contractions began in earnest, my parents rushed to the hospital in time to see the New Year ushered in. I was delivered at 12:34 a.m. and named Judith Evelyn Briggs.

I was born into a loud, colorful, gregarious Irish/English family with parents and siblings who loved each other and me. My mother's name was Lillian Kathleen Turner Briggs, born on July 27, 1905, in Belfast, Ireland, the first child of James and Isabel Turner. They emigrated from Ireland shortly after she was born and settled in Winnipeg, Manitoba. After my mother, they had five more children: three girls and two boys.

James Turner, my maternal grandfather, was a streetcar driver who always told us that he was related to George Bernard Shaw through his Irish roots. (I would like to do more investigation into the family tree and check this out for myself.)

My grandmother, Isabella, was a cook in a castle, reminiscent of *Downtown Abbey's* Daisy—or at least that's the way I like to imagine her. I never had the opportunity to meet her, since she died of cancer before I was born.

John Russell Briggs, my father, was born on the farm in Cereal (yes, Cereal!), Alberta, in 1906, the oldest of seven siblings. His mother was a tailor and his father, my grandfather, was a farmer/politician like his own father.

I have a portrait of my great-grandfather, who served as an MP (Member of Parliament) in the province of Manitoba for thirty-three years. To my grandchildren, this man, William Briggs, would be your great-great-great-grandfather—three greats!

My father's family had been in Canada for generations. In fact, my ancestors had traveled as United Empire Loyalists to what was then British North America.

A note of history: Loyalists were American colonists who supported the British cause during the American Revolution (1775–83). Tens of thousands migrated to British North America during and after the revolutionary war —increasing the population and shaping the politics and culture of what would become Canada.

According to the Canadian Encyclopedia, "Sympathy for the Crown was a dangerous sentiment: those who defied the revolutionary forces could find themselves without civil rights, subject to mob violence, or flung into prison. Loyalist property was vandalized and often confiscated.

"During the Revolution more than 19,000 Loyalists served Britain in specially created provincial militia corps, accompanied by several thousand Aboriginal allies. Others spent the war in such strongholds as New York City and Boston, or in refugee camps such as those at Sorel and Machiche, Québec. Between 80,000 and 100,000 eventually fled, about half of them to Canada."[3]

My father's ancestors, the Loyalists, arrived in Eastern Canada and then traveled by covered wagon many miles to eventually settle as pioneers in the frontier of Western Canada. Maybe that's why I have such an interest in, and a loyalty to, all things British Royal Family, getting up in the middle of the night to watch all the royal weddings.

The Briggs family brought music with them from the old country. According to my father, he and his family members were all musical, to the point where they would bring their fiddles, mandolins, accordions and guitars to provide music for the local Friday night barn dances. My grandfather, William, an exceptional fiddler, led the way on these convivial evenings.

My dad loved talking about those old times, making music with his family. They didn't have much money, but they were rich in music and derived great pleasure from it, as I still do. My dad and my sister Barb and I had many fun times going to fiddling events in Ontario as we were growing up

The Briggs family descendants still relish the chance to make music together. In 2007, my cousin, Donald Russell, came for a visit to Grand Rapids. He and his sisters all play the fiddle, guitar, mandolin, and banjo, and they all sing and write songs.

I was reluctant when Don suggested I get out my old violin and learn to fiddle. Let's just say I didn't want to subject the two of us to my squeaks after years of not playing. With a little coaxing, I agreed, and I got out my violin and started playing.

What fun to play music together in the great Briggs family tradition! Inspired by my cousin's encouragement, I continued with violin, now as a member of a swing band and occasionally with a worship band at church.

My violin is a treasured possession. My father gave me his antique violin, the same one that he played in the *Winnipeg Symphony Orchestra* in the early 1920s, when this violin was already one hundred years

---

3 *Loyalists*, www.thecanadianencyclopedia.ca

old. As the story goes, this violin came all the way from Germany, made by a German violin maker. Now this beautiful instrument, almost two hundred years old, still makes music and brings me pleasure in the playing of it.

When I opened my violin case after many years, I rediscovered a sweet note from my father: "I am giving you my most cherished possession," he wrote. "I hope you will continue to play your instrument to the glory of God."

With a pang, I realized there had been no glory coming from that violin for far too long. My father's note sparked a desire in me to start up again and keep playing.

Music was foundational in our family. In fact, it would end up being the matchmaker for my parents. When my father played violin in the *Winnipeg Symphony Orchestra* in the early 1920s, his stand partner was George Turner, my mother's younger brother. When George brought his tall, handsome friend home for dinner, both my grandmother and my mother fell instantly in love with him.

By the time I was born in 1944, I already had several siblings. My sister Joyce Isabel was twelve, my brother William James "Jimmy" was ten, and my brother Russell Bruce, whom we called Bruce, was six when I arrived. My younger sister Barbara Joanne was born when I was four-and-a-half, in the hot summer of 1948.

I have a vague memory of being at our summer cottage on Lake Simcoe, fussing and fretting about the whereabouts and well-being of my mother. She had been in the hospital in Toronto, enduring a long, drawn-out labor at the age of 44, so I guess my father wanted to distract the rest of us and brought us up to the cottage to cool off.

Unfortunately for him, I was having none of his tactics, and kicked up such a fuss that he brought us all back from the cottage an hour away. I was so worried about my mother and my soon-to-be-born baby sibling! But all was well, and my mother soon came home with her newest Briggs member.

I think from that time on, I felt some responsibility to take care of my baby sister—even as adults when she was more than capable of taking care of herself. As adults we talked about that when I was too bossy or overpowering, and she had no trouble setting me straight. I sure wish she was still here.

We sold the cottage soon after Barb was born. It had nothing to do with her arrival and everything to do with my mother not wanting to cook and clean endlessly for all the business guests my father invited to the cottage. But we did occasionally go back to that lake. I always loved to swim, especially with my dad.

He was an enormous man, in girth and personality, and he would swim out to the deeper parts of the lake and often float, serving as a human raft for us kids. I'm sure it was quite the sight for all the cottagers: all of his 6 ft. 4 in, 400-pound self. For me though, it was also quite a happy memory.

As I got older, however, I was really embarrassed by my father's size. I believe now in looking back that my father suffered from a biological depression and medicated himself with food. Back then in the 1950s and 60s we didn't know of medical interventions for depression or anxiety.

With Barb's birth, the Briggs family was complete. Life at 212 Wanless Avenue was full of many things: lots of fun, spontaneity, laughter, and large regular family gatherings around a dining room table laden with delicious food.

However, there was also an underlying tension, mostly due to my parents fighting over the lack of money and my father's inability to pay our basic bills. There were outbursts of angry name calling which sometimes became physical towards my mother and older siblings.

Thankfully that behavior stopped as I grew older. However, having observed these episodes early on, I decided it was safer to avoid the anger/conflict by being a "good girl."

There always seemed to be lots of food, no matter how little money there was to pay the bills. I remember sitting at the dining room table almost every night for a full course family meal. In retrospect I know that my mother was an expert in creativity and managed what we had available quite adeptly.

Those evening meals and the food became a comfort in the chaos—an ingrained stronghold for me that I still feel is a challenge. The problems for the time being seemed to disappear with the panacea of the food.

Mixed in with all the chaos, in addition to the fun and celebration, there was music and lots of it, enhanced by love and affection. Both of my parents were quite emotional and had no trouble showing their emotions, positive and negative! I knew from the beginning that I was loved and it was regularly communicated to me.

In our own marriage, Steve wrote a letter to me when we were going through a rough spot, in which he said, "Even though your family was chaotic, they knew how to love each other." I am very grateful for that love which has enabled me to love easily. Steve loved my family and they dearly loved him.

Our home, a 1920s red brick Tudor revival, was close to a park where we skated and tobogganed in the winter and played tennis and baseball in the summer. There were lots of children in our neighborhood to play with in all seasons.

In the winter we behaved like the Canadian children we were and skated and played hockey until we couldn't feel our limbs. There was a skating rink and a hockey rink at Wanless Park, and sometimes we girls played hockey with the boys when they were short of players.

Some years my father and brothers flooded our backyard, which adjoined other neighbors' flooded backyards. This created a winding trail of ice for us on which to play and glide. On New Year's Eve the neighborhood would host a party for all the neighbors, and we kids could chase each other around and through our back yards on skates. This would be topped off with hot chocolate, popcorn, and lots of laughter, and I'm sure "hot toddies" for the parents.

Winter, spring, summer, and fall, when it was time to come in for dinner, my mother rang the big old school bell and we had to respond by calling out, "coming!" I still have that old bell, by the way. It seems to reverberate with my mother's admonition to hurry and return home. Dinner was ready!

We lived within walking distance of school and the unique, artsy stores on Yonge Street. I still relish the chance to go back there to walk by my old house, down my old streets, and remember. I guess I'm just quite sentimental! And, yes, getting old, now ¾ of a century. How different it is now in our present culture of fear: children walking to school alone, and playing outside all day until dark.

Another favorite memory was walking down to the Roslin Store, a neighborhood mom and pop shop which sold scrumptious penny candy—black balls, licorice pipes, strawberry marshmallows, and on and on. We didn't always have extra money for penny candy, so we had to become entrepreneurial.

During lazy summer months we would collect coat hangers (which we would "cash in" at the local dry cleaner for one penny per hanger) and glass pop bottles to fund candy and popsicles on sweltering days. For additional funds we would organize frequent lemonade stands on the street corners.

One peculiar activity: I remember sitting on the curb taking down license plate numbers and recording them in neat columns on a piece of paper. Back in the day I thought it was fun, but for the life of me, now I can't imagine why! Maybe that's why I still like to make lists.

We took a big road trip one summer from Toronto to the prairie country outside of Winnipeg to visit my Aunt Dora (my father's sister) and Uncle Donald on the farm. I was about ten or eleven, and fifteen-year-old Bruce and five-year-old Barb were along as well. There were oohs and aahs around the table as we dug into homegrown vegetables, strawberries and cream, homemade bread, and home-churned butter.

Our house with three and a half bedrooms and one bathroom was sufficient for all seven of us (what you don't know can't hurt you). I learned to play the piano and paint pictures. One of my most cherished Christmas presents ever was a paint-by-number set. I sat at the little desk in the living room and blissfully painted for the whole Christmas day.

Later, as a grown-up living in Banff, I took up art lessons and painted with Deborah every afternoon when she came home from kindergarten. After Steve died, a friend took me to watercolor classes, which I loved.

In the living room, we gathered to listen to the radio. Television had not yet been invented, and in fact we did not have one in our home until I was a teenager. We'd gather round the 1954 Lowe Opta Luna radio, with its wooden frame and gold trim, leaning in to catch every word of "Ma and Pa Kettle" and "Hi Ho Silver."

As a small child I tried to figure out how the radio worked. *Were there miniature people with little instruments inside this big wooden box making music?* I wondered. Concrete thinking at its best.

My mother loved to cook but didn't really like housework. So our job as kids was to complete most of the cleaning on Saturdays. Barb and I would take turns doing the upstairs or the downstairs alternatively. Because I liked to work fast and get it over with and Barb liked to procrastinate, I solved that dilemma by alternating floors.

I'm sure Barb did a more thorough cleaning job than me. She could take as long as she wanted to do her cleaning and I could zip through my floor quickly to get on to the next thing. Barb and I joked about that later as adults. Even though we were different in many ways, we loved each other intensely.

I miss her love and friendship a lot, now that she died, oh so young. In fact, even writing this now after several years, there are tears in my eyes. My sisters and I were the very best of friends and we always talked about how blessed we were.

My mother boasted other strengths besides cooking. She had a warm, hospitable, party-loving heart and was always reaching out to people. My parents at their best were kind and generous people. If someone needed a meal, a bed, or clothes they knew where to come.

A funny story about that: One day my father brought a homeless man home to give him food and clothes. He went to my brother Bruce's closet and gave this man a pair of new shoes that Bruce had just bought with his own money—because they fit him! Can you imagine the fireworks that went on in our house because of that incident?

Mom never did learn to drive but, as I said, she was a fabulous cook and spent hours each day in the kitchen. We kids would come home to the tantalizing aroma of cookies, muffins, pies, and butter tarts. Her specialty was banana crème pie, and I can still taste the creamy, sweet filling.

My father also liked to cook. He would make homemade tomato soup from scratch, and on Sunday morning, he would cook a roast beef dinner for the rest of us when we arrived home from church. As long as my mother wasn't looking, he would let us dip a piece of bread on the bottom of the roasting pan before the gravy was made. "Bread dip," we called it. Delectable and delicious, especially since we had to sneak it!

At times, my mother was plagued with arthritic back pain, and was bedridden sometimes for several weeks at a time. One time when the house was in disarray and we were all sad and grumpily disorganized, I stayed home from school to take care of her and organize the house. I think I must have been in third grade.

In response, my brother, Bruce, went up to Yonge Street and purchased with his own money a gift of a belt in the latest fashion to say thank you. He even bought a card, which said, "Thanks for helping, Mom." This memory shines for me because Bruce was never one to throw around compliments or praise, especially to me as his little sister.

In fact, if he told me something like, "You'll never be able to ski," that was enough motivation for me to learn to ski. But Bruce and I had fun together too. It was our job to do the dishes after a humongous family meal. We'd sing and harmonize, the Everly Brothers, Elvis Presley, Pat Boone, and Beach Boy songs while twirling around our tea towels. It took us a long time to get the dishes done!

In fact, one time when the school principal asked my brother why he didn't do his homework, he replied. "Sir, I didn't have time; I had to do the dishes." We all got a laugh out of that one. Bruce excelled at all sports but didn't appreciate scholastics, even though he was very smart.

When my mother was well, she pulled out the stops to make life festive and fun. I think of the "graduation party" that my mom threw for me when I graduated from kindergarten. In retrospect I think she was just having a luncheon for some of her friends, but since it was my last day of school, she called it a graduation party. She loved to celebrate.

In my mind, I hear her at the piano, pounding out some made-up march while we children, plus an assortment of our friends, marched around with our orchestra of pots and pans. It was my first experience in an orchestra and it was love at first sound.

Once three of my girlfriends and I practiced a quartet with my mother at the piano. We sang the old classic "Jerusalem" in four-part harmony. My mother, who was hopelessly biased, thought that we were as good as the Lennon Sisters and that we should audition for *The Ed Sullivan Show*. Of course, we believed her and started to imagine what it would be like to be TV stars, singing together in matching dresses, soaking in all the attention and fame.

Recently, these same girl friends and I who have kept in touch, reminisced about those dreams. Gaynor, Gussie, Mary, and I were the wannabe Lennon Sisters. We've kept in touch all of these years. Two of us went on to become professional musicians, just didn't make TV fame.

Oh, the dreams! Mom was an accomplished pianist as well, reading music, but playing anything she heard from ear. She passed that love of piano playing on to me for sure.

My mother would seize upon any excuse at all to celebrate. When our cat, Twinkle, delivered kittens in what seemed like the middle of the night, my mother woke us up out of a sound sleep and we commemorated the happy news by baking a cake. Funnily it was called a "Twinkle Mix".

When those kittens were several weeks old, we had a "christening party" for all the children and mothers in the neighborhood, complete with handmade invitations. On the menu were dainty tea sandwiches and pink lemonade. We dressed the kittens up in little doll bonnets and dress clothes (despite their desperate mewing), and nestled them in our doll buggies for the "christening."

I was the officiating minister, and I delegated the parental roles to my sister and to my best friend and next-door neighbor, Peter Ketchie. The ceremony was a huge success, and afterward we feasted on the sandwiches. The kittens were thrilled, of course. Not!

Cat Miracles

While we are on the topic of cats, I must tell you the story of Twinkle's inexplicable return. When she was just a kitten herself, she went missing, much to my devastation. My mother was a brand-new Christian at the time, and she led us all in praying diligently for Twinkle's safe return.

A few days after this prayer, there was a knock on the door at nighttime. We opened the door to behold a man holding a kitten in his hands. "Does this little kitten belong to you?" he asked. Did she ever! What rejoicing to have our Twinkle back and what praising God for answering our prayers!

Mom was so excited about her simple Christian faith. She taught us to pray about everything, a modeling for which I am grateful. Another *miracle*, at least to me.

"Cat miracles" have continued in our family lore. Fast forward twenty-six years later, and I was married with two children ages eight and nine. Pumpkin, our beloved cat, had disappeared on Halloween night. Little Debbie especially was beyond comfort.

We called the Humane Society, posted missing cat posters on poles around the neighborhood and followed up on various leads, only to be sorely disappointed. And we prayed, just as my mother had led me to do as a child. Yet there was no sign of our Pumpkin.

About six weeks later, I told Debbie to stop praying for Pumpkin's return. I thought the cat was gone for good. "She probably was in cat heaven," I said. I was tired of following up on fruitless leads to no avail. Oh, me of little faith!

Then one of my friends called me with a bit of news. A teacher from the local school had been heard talking about a cat she'd found. I figured it was another false lead. *I'll try one more time*, I thought, without much hope.

I went and got the cat, and called Steve to meet me at the front door to help me confirm whether this was Pumpkin with her distinctive orange tabby streak on her tail. After all, it had been 6 weeks for her to grow and I knew that she would look different.

I had the cat tucked under my parka when I rang the front doorbell so only Steve would answer that door. I really didn't want to get my hopes up, but this cat sure seemed like our lost cat. Deb came running to the door and saw the cat's orange tabby streaked-tail hanging out from under my parka.

"Pumpkin!" she cried out. "God did answer my prayers. Even though you told me to stop praying, Mommy, I didn't!" She grabbed Pumpkin and I'm sure you could hear the purr from both of them across town.

My daughter had more faith than I did. Here was our precious cat that went on to enjoy eighteen more hearty years of life with us. She eventually reached "catzeimers" age and we had to send her to heaven. It was another instance of God caring for us in a detailed, personal way.

Since I'm on a roll here, may I tell you one more story about cats and miracles—a theme, it seems in our family? A few years ago, I received a sad call from my daughter, Deb. Deborah was now a grown woman and married with three children. Their adored cat, Callie, had been found dead in the neighbor's yard, killed by some other animal.

Deb and her family were crushed to lose their Callie, one of four wild kittens they had found outside in their garage, abandoned by their mother. Deb and the kids had tamed them, loved them, spoke life into their little fearful eyes, and ultimately taught them to trust. Eventually, they gave two away but kept two: Callie and Gus.

Not long after Callie's demise, Gus disappeared. This time, there was heightened grief and fear that Gus had met the same grisly end as his sister. Deb called me and asked me to pray. The family posted signs, followed up on tips, and basically exerted lots of energy trying to find their Gus. The weeks wore on, but no Gus.

One evening, after the kids had a bit of a meltdown regarding their lost pets, Deb decided enough was enough. "I think we might have to accept the fact that Gus may not be coming back, but let's pray one more time that, if Gus is still alive, he will come back quickly," Deb said.

She prayed. "If Gus is still alive, Lord, would you bring him back right away?"

That night, the family was in bed sleeping except for Deb's husband, Kent, who was doing some paperwork in his home office. Suddenly, he heard a loud meow outside, and behold—it was the long-lost Gus! Kent was so excited that he woke the family up and they, Gus's entire family, hugged and cried and cheered at his homecoming.

From Twinkle to Pumpkin to Gus—we've experienced a kind of generational blessing when it comes to cats lost and found. Three generations, three cats, three praying mothers and their faithful praying children.

***

I've already told you a bit about the beginning of my faith journey. My parents were Christmas/Easter churchgoers. (My mother became a Christian when I was about twelve years old.)

Children perceive so much more than the adults give them credit for, and I perceived fear and depression and anxiety underneath the externals of our family life. I had been born near the latter part of World War II, which ended when I was twenty-one months old, on

September 2, 1945. Several years later, there was still lingering anxiety in the air about the possibility of being attacked.

Fears about the Russians bombing us (whether real or imagined), coupled with the constant angst in our house over how we would pay our bills, had plunged me into a mess of worry and fright. I've already told you about the tension in our family regarding finances.

Whenever we verbalized our concerns about money, my dad would say, "Don't worry, I'll just go in the basement and open another barrel of money." He was good at denial. It became kind of a family joke as we grew up and had our own families, the "barrel of money" metaphor.

I already described (see *Introduction*) how I cried out to Jesus one night, not even knowing about God, and how I saw him at the foot of my bed assuring me that He would never leave me or forsake me.

God intervened in the life of a scared small girl. I knew in that moment I could trust him to respond to me. I felt his love for the first time and it calmed me. Many a time over the last seventy years when I am fearful and feeling insecure and lonely, I go back to that vision of Jesus and remember his life-giving Word to me.

Through all the changes and transitions in my life, the security of knowing Jesus and experiencing his comforting presence has sustained me. And it all started that day with a cry of the heart: *"Jesus, help me!"*

It was the first miracle in my life, but by no means was it the last.

Musing

I'm so thankful that I have experienced God's comforting presence, love, and help throughout my life. How about you?

Chapter 2

A Miracle of Conversion

Trust in the Lord with all your heart and lean not on your own understanding. In all your ways acknowledge Him and He will direct your path (Proverbs 3:5,6).

At age 11 in 1955, I committed my life in a public way to follow Jesus. There has been no turning back since that time.

When I was eleven years old, I heard that Billy Graham was coming to Toronto for something called a "crusade." I wanted to go, I think, because my brother Jim seemed to be a fan of Billy Graham and would listen to him on the radio.

My mother let me go downtown to Maple Leaf Gardens with a couple of my girlfriends, Betsy and Gaynor. We took the bus and subway, quite an adventure. Of course, in those days we were perfectly safe.

I listened intently as Reverend Graham preached the Gospel. He had made it very clear: "The Bible says: If you repent of your sins and believe that Jesus died and was resurrected, and if you ask Jesus into your heart, He will forgive you and be with you forever."

I was ready to open my heart and give my life to Jesus. The Holy Spirit was graciously drawing me to himself and I responded. When the call was issued to come forward as a public sign of my new faith, I knew I had to go forward. With my heart beating madly, I walked forward solemnly with a throng of other new Christians.

Of course, I made my girlfriends come with me down the aisle, regardless of their own decisions. Was it the beginning of my evangelistic leanings? Probably, although not the best method, I am sure.

Fast forward to forty years later: I heard that Billy Graham was going to give another crusade in Toronto. I wanted to go. It felt like a spiritual journey of gratitude for that life-saving decision I had made forty years before.

At that time there was a direct flight from Grand Rapids to Toronto. As it turned out, I was the only passenger on the plane. What a blast! My own private plane transporting me to say thank you to God for my life.

Bedford Park Elementary School

Bedford Park School was located about two and a half blocks along Wanless Avenue, the same street on which I lived. I always walked to school, usually with friends who would meet me at the corner of Ronan and Wanless.

School and learning was almost always a good thing for me. My academic career improved after an inauspicious start, coming home from school on the first day of grade one, a puddle of tears because I couldn't read. (My mother assured me things would be fine, that I was enrolled in Grade One precisely to learn to read!) I apparently learned to read—reading is still one of my favorite pastimes.

In Grade Five, I enjoyed being a part of the Audubon club, a bird club led by our teacher, Miss Turner. She would take us on early morning bird hikes in the local parks before school where we would eagerly try and spot cardinals, blue jays, robins, sparrows, and woodpeckers.

Each Friday afternoon we held our official meeting, and as president of the class, I was called upon to deliver a speech. "Miss Turner, classmates, and fellow citizens," I began …

I would struggle and worry over these speeches each week, with my mother helping me write them out at lunchtime. Back then we had an hour and a half for our lunch break. That three-minute speech felt like a giant responsibility.

Would I have been reassured if I had known then that I would go on to deliver countless speeches, seminars, and teachings to groups of all sizes? Probably not. I would have been more frightened. Maybe God was preparing me for future ministry?

Clearly, God was not preparing me for a life as the first female draft pick for the Toronto Blue Jays, but I also enjoyed playing and pitching softball during those years. As captain of the team, I would gather my teammates for prayer before each game, to ask for a win. (I must admit I don't know how sound that theology is.)

I also competed in some track and field events and won a prize once—and only once, be assured—for the "hop, step, and jump" (similar to long jump) event at a track meet. My only explanation for this unexpected sporting triumph was that I was tall for my age and had long legs.

Being found notable for a sporting event was not the usual, but thriving in music was a consistent, golden thread that would weave through my entire life. I had so much fun making music, especially at Christmas when the choirs and ensembles and string instruments would put on their major concerts and we would sing carols through the halls of our elementary school.

Those of us who took music classes had to wear short navy tunics and white blouses at all our performances with our music award crests sewn into the tunics. In school our choirs, triple trios, and orchestras competed at the Kiwanis Festival, which held citywide concerts at the great old Massey Hall. The budding performer in me was greatly encouraged.

At home on Wanless Avenue, music was encouraged from the cradle onward. I began taking violin lessons in Grade Three, and whenever we had company, my dad would insist that my sister Barb and I play the piano or the violin or both for the company. He was so proud of us, although I can't help but wonder how the company felt about these impromptu concerts foisted upon them.

Well, at least those little concerts helped build my performing confidence. Sometimes Barb and I would play violin duets, with our mother accompanying us on the piano for services at the downtown Scott Mission for the homeless. Barb stayed with the violin and became a much better violinist than me.

Fast forward 55 years. When Barb was dying, we reminisced about those duets at the Mission when we would first play the violin together, then sing a duet. What an amazing memory for me when we sang together during her last days on earth and harmonized again on that old hymn, "Now wash me and I shall be whiter than snow."

Barb's daughter, Jenny, made a recording of our song together—such a precious gift now that Barb is in heaven.

I also took piano lessons from Mr. Harold Patterson at the Toronto Conservatory of Music for two dollars per lesson. (Two dollars in the mid-fifties roughly equals around eighteen to twenty dollars in today's currency.) Mom saved glass milk bottles to pay for those lessons, which strikes me as wonderfully capable and frugal. She would be glad to know her resourcefulness paid off, and I still love playing the piano to this day.

Joyce inherited the piano because she lived close by. When the family sorted out her house after she passed, I had that special piano shipped to me at my lake house. When I sat down to play it again for the first time, it was like the piano and my fingers remembered each other.

Back at Bedford Park School, I managed to make it all the way to Grade Eight before being sent down to the principal's office. It had been snowing heavily, and perhaps I was a bit restless that day. Someone dared me to open the window and make a snowball and then throw it—inside, across the room to one of the boys on whom I had a crush.

Apparently, the temptation was too much for me, and I threw open the window sash and quickly scooped a gleaming white ball of snow. With uncanny timing, the teacher reappeared at the very moment I heaved the snowball across Mr. McAdam's classroom. Uh-oh.

My cheeks burned hot with shame as I marched down to the principal's office. I had never been in trouble before, so I was stepping into unknown territory. Inside the principal's office, I received a scathing rebuke—one I have obviously never forgotten all these years later!

I had to stay in his office and write the words, "I will never throw a snowball in class again," one hundred times. I chuckle at the memory now because I was so intimidated. It felt like the end of the world had come. I was *so* scared.

The snowball misdemeanor notwithstanding, I won the cup in Grade Eight for the "most all-round girl," an award for the female student who excelled across academics, sports, and music. At home, everyone was beaming, especially my mother. I'm sure that she encouraged me toward that goal and probably prayed it into being.

I do remember being very surprised and almost embarrassed when it actually happened. I have a copy of the photo of me that hung in the school for some years. It marked the first time I had my hair professionally done at the hairdresser and that's what I remembered.

Speaking of getting all dolled up, I was becoming a young woman (Grade Eight) and growing more interested in the opposite sex. That year, Friday nights took on an extra appeal, as there were square dancing nights at the school.

We had all learned to square dance in the all-female gym class at school and, because I was so tall for my age, I always had to be the boy. Hence when I was dancing with a boy, my instinct was to lead, which often led to me tripping over my feet—and his. But those Friday nights glow in memory as being great fun.

When I wasn't square dancing, my girlfriends and I would go to one girl's house (who boasted a television while the rest of us still just had radios). We'd all curl up in front of her 21-inch console television set, with its mahogany-finish and boxy wood frame on four squat legs. Can you just picture it?

Our favorite show was *Mama*, a family drama about a Norwegian family living in San Francisco at the turn of the twentieth century. We'd pop big bowls of buttery popcorn and enjoy an entire 8 oz. bottle of Coke all to ourselves—the height of decadence. (We usually had to share a bottle at home.)

However, the Elvis concert was truly the height of decadence (tickets provided by my rich friend's parents.). It was April 2 (unbeknown to me, my future husband's birthday), 1957, at Maple Leaf Gardens. I was thirteen years old and closer to Elvis Presley than most people ever got.

It was the first concert Elvis had ever performed in Canada, and my girlfriend's parents had gotten us two tickets in or near the front row. Elvis just seemed so close when he came out on stage!

I screamed my head off and waved my arms like everyone else to his hits such as "Hound Dog." And we all swayed in time to "Love Me Tender," which I still think is an achingly lovely song. I've always loved Elvis's music. It's so sad that he, like so many other talented, creative stars, suffered such a tragic demise.

A tender memory I have of Elvis's music happened two weeks

before Steve died. We were at a wedding, and Steve and I won the prize for the only couple left on the dance floor as we cuddle-shuffled around to the music, "Love Me Tender."

A piece of my Grade Eight year—such an important "hinge" between childhood and high school and beyond—is commemorated on my wall in the form of a butterfly poster. I had missed a science exam due to sickness. In retrospect I think it was anxiety because I remember my mother taking me to a doctor and the doctor prescribing a tiny little pill (anti-anxiety pill?). I don't know.

I was often anxious about exams and performance and would over prepare for everything. Anyway, I was given the chance to make up the exam by creating a poster about butterflies. My dad helped me with the assignment and was so proud of how it had turned out, he had it professionally sprayed with some sort of substance to protect it and had it framed.

I rescued this "piece of art" from my family home after my mother died. We never imagined just how much longevity it would have. The poster hangs downstairs in my lake condo, hung at some point because Steve and Parker both loved butterflies. It's old and cracked now, but I guess we can give it some grace. It's sixty years old, after all.

Art? That's questionable. Longevity, certainly so.

Joyce and Dag

When I was twelve years old, my big sister Joyce got married. Now, Joyce was more than a sister to me. She really was a second mother, and a wonderful one at that. She comforted me when I was sad, taught me when I needed teaching, and took care of me in many, many ways.

Joyce taught me about the birds and the bees, bought me clothes, and took me for my first haircut. My long hair, which had always been French braided by my mom was transformed into a cute pageboy. Joyce had much to do with the shaping of who I became as an adult. I could never have repaid her for the constant love and encouragement she lavished on me for my entire life. What a gift.

And as I write this, I still miss her *soooo* much. As adults we shared our hearts and secrets, sometimes on a daily basis, as I also did with

Barb. And we prayed for each other. Having sisters as your best friends was certainly a blessing and we talked about that fact often.

As a giant bonus, Joyce married Dag (a nickname for Jerry), who became my beloved brother. The family couldn't afford a big wedding in those days, so Joyce and Dag were married in the East Chapel of Timothy Eaton Memorial Church.

Situated in the heart of Toronto, the 1914 church is made of stone and has the feel of a cathedral with stained glass windows and a 7,000-pipe organ. (In later years, Joyce became an elder there.) Because she and Dag's wedding was such a small affair, they opted for the intimacy of the chapel. Only nine people attended, and the only other sibling there was Jimmy—he was the designated photographer.

Many decades later, Dag's funeral service graced the main auditorium and I had the honor of singing "The Lord's Prayer" and "Because He Lives."

Dag was closer than a brother to me. He patiently helped me with my homework, and I cheered him on as he pitched for his baseball team. Often Barb and I would spend weekends at Joyce and Dag's apartment, where we'd make cookies and do all sorts of fun things. Joyce and Dag were a beautiful, striking couple. He was tall, dark, and handsome (really), and she was gorgeous, also tall and lithe with aristocratic high cheekbones and a flair for fashion.

When John, my first nephew, was about to be born, his mother, Joyce, was at our house on Wanless Avenue. As I sat by her bedside, I timed her labor pains until it was decided that she be taken to the hospital. In those days, fathers-to-be did not enter the delivery room, so Dag waited it out with us back at home. He sat by the telephone, with Barb and I sitting on the steps behind him.

We were thrilled when baby John entered the world. Barb and I would often baby-sit our adorable little nephew and became very close to him.

Joyce and Dag were married for forty-two years until he was stricken with Mesothelioma, which apparently came from his exposure to asbestos when he served in the Canadian Navy on a submarine during World War II. A couple of weeks before he died, I drove from Grand Rapids to Toronto to say goodbye to my marvelous bonus brother.

With laborious effort, dear weak Dag got himself up and dressed and waited for me for hours on their front porch. We loved each other dearly, and I asked him to save us a house close to his when he went to heaven. He died in 1998 and dear Joyce 13 years later. How I miss them both.

My Mother's Conversion: A Miracle

My mother's conversion was another big hinge moment in our family's life. There was a *before* and an *after*, two distinct epochs in the Briggs' history.

One big change in the *after* was that we started attending Danforth Gospel Temple, a church in the PAOC (Pentecostal Assemblies of Canada). It would end up being my church home up to the point of my marriage to Steve, at which time we moved away.

Dr. J. Harry Faught was our pastor for years until 1968 when he moved to Calgary. In the book, *Aspects of the Canadian Evangelical Experience*, the author writes of Pastor Faught, "He established a reputation in Toronto as an articulate spokesman, not only for the Pentecostals but for Evangelicalism, commenting on current social, religious, and political events."[4]

That's the way I remember him, as bringing a blend of Pentecostalism and good, solid thinking and theology to the pulpit. He had graduated from the conservative Dallas Theological Seminary with a doctorate in philosophy, yet had retained his beliefs about the gifts of the Spirit.

I remember Pastor Faught, who taught our college-age group Sunday school class, was always there to listen and answer any questions about faith we might have. We as young people felt the freedom to grapple with our doubts and come to terms with them. In fact, he encouraged us to ask questions. He often said, "Tell your questions to God and ask him to show you the answers."

We came to Danforth in a roundabout way, via two new friends, George and Flo Owens, whom my parents met at a different church entirely. God surely brought them together that evening to work out his purposes.

---

4 *Aspects of the Canadian Evangelical Experience,* McGill-Queen's University Press; 1 edition (February 17, 1997), edited by G.A. Rawlyk

On the Sunday night my parents met George and Flo, Mom and Dad decided to attend a small independent gospel church nearby for the first—and last—time. My parents were sporadic churchgoers at best, attending a staid United Church on holiday occasions. The story begins with my parents' anxiety about a visitor arriving in Toronto from Winnipeg over a weekend.

"He's an Evangelical and might raise his hands in a worship service," my mother fretted. "He'll expect us to take him to church on Sunday, but we certainly can't take him to our church. He'll be sure to embarrass us if he raises his hands or shouts 'Amen' or 'Hallelujah.'"

My parents consulted the phone book and found this church that they knew nothing about and they would know no one. Meanwhile, across the city, George and Flo were "listening to the Lord" and had this strange unction to attend this same church on a Sunday night. They also had never been there. God was orchestrating a meeting with eternity in mind.

That night, at this little church, my parents avoided embarrassment with their United Church friends, who were not present to witness the Winnipegger raising his hands. But they could not avoid the Holy Spirit.

At church, George and Flo noticed this family of four children, all dressed to impress, sitting in the last row. Led by the Spirit, they approached us and invited my teenage brothers to a young people's party, which had just been announced from the pulpit. They also offered to come to our home to pick up the boys for the event.

I don't remember whether my brothers went or not, but the Owens's must have become friendly with my parents too. My next memory is hearing my mother weeping. George had just shared the Gospel with her, and she knelt on the living room floor by that old faded green chesterfield, and accepted Jesus as her personal Savior.

God was moving in my family. I had already received Jesus as my Lord, and now my mother followed suit, dropping to her knees with a hungry heart to accept the Bread of Life. My mother was transformed.

She had been a smoker for years, but the next morning she wondered if she should keep smoking in light of her new identity as a believer. A *miracle*?

"God, please show me somehow if I should quit smoking," she prayed, standing by the kitchen sink. As she told the story, "My hand then began to shake so hard that I dropped the cigarette into the sink and it bounced in the drain. That was the last cigarette I ever smoked." Her addiction to nicotine was broken.

Another disclaimer: I don't believe if a person smokes that they're not a Christian. That's kind of legalistic and I don't think it has anything to do with the gospel. However, it was a simple question my mother asked. We do know now that smoking isn't good for your health at least.

Early in her faith journey my mother grasped the power of prayer, becoming a mighty prayer warrior and interceding for our family in every situation, big or small. In fact, the night after she had become a Christian, my mother opened her mouth to pray and began to praise God in tongues, a heavenly language and one of the gifts of the Spirit. She didn't even know about this gift at the time. More about that gift of the Holy Spirit later.

Mom taught me to pray about everything. We prayed together to find a lost library book, and before school and club speeches, presentations, tests, and exams. She prayed for me as I led our baseball team in prayer before our games, and when I was stood up for a date in college.

She mediated for me when I might be under spiritual attack, such as the time I recited Psalm 23 in front of my classroom, choosing it as my spoken piece of poetry to witness to my classmates. Mom would get up very early to pray, kneeling by the large, green French provincial sofa in the living room, with her Bible and hymnbook open.

When she died from a stroke and Alzheimer's disease in 1990, even though her brain was scrambled, she still responded to the familiar music of the old hymns. Her spirit, which was still intact, knew the words from heart.

Sometimes the stakes were high as far as our earthly well-being. One time, we didn't have funds in our bank to pay our house mortgage (many months' worth), and we had no idea where that money was coming from. We would lose the house if we couldn't pay that month and didn't have any other place to go.

I remember my mother calling me into her room to pray. She was so upset. We both knelt by the bed, and we prayed fervently together that God would somehow provide. We were literally on our knees when the phone rang. It was my Grandfather Turner, from Winnipeg, my mother's father, whom she hadn't spoken to for some time.

He had cut her off when he learned that she had taken up smoking. At least that's how the story goes, but I know there must have been more to it than that. My grandfather offered to lend us $8,000 so that we could keep our house. My father did repay him much later, when he sold his business and the downtown building that housed it.

This phone call in answer to our prayers brought about reconciliation. Grandfather Turner began to visit us regularly and even ended up living with us in his later years when he had Alzheimer's disease. Another *miracle*? Certainly an answer to our prayers, and, yes, to me it was a *miracle*.

My mother also taught me how to pray for her. On one occasion she called out to me in a panic, to come to her bedside. "Pray for me," she begged. "I think I am dying!"

Now that I am a mental health professional, I look back and think that she must have been having a panic attack—one of the symptoms of an anxiety disorder, which is "the fear of impending doom." In any event, I obeyed my mother's wish and prayed for her, after which she quickly calmed down and went back to sleep. I must have been pretty scared but seeing my mother's calming response was a comfort and a lesson for me back then, I guess.

Mom's penchant for prayer in all things was such a gift to her children. Her intercession for us continued until she became sick with the Alzheimer's disease. Maybe she still prayed, even then. She certainly responded to praise music, even when she couldn't remember any of us, nor could she speak anything intelligible.

One blessing for me happened just before her death. We had driven up from Michigan to Toronto for one of many visits to see her. As I knelt by her wheelchair and put my head on her lap to say goodbye, she said, while stroking my head, "You're a darling, "D A R L I N G." I will never forget that. She must have known that she was confused and spelled the word out to make sure I would get the message. Thank you, Lord Jesus.

Danforth Gospel Temple: My Church

Sunday school and youth group at Danforth Gospel Church became a core part of my life, spiritually shaping me and who I would become. This was the home church of our new Christian friends, George and Flo Owens.

In Grade Nine there was one of many contests held to see who could bring the most people to Sunday school. (These competitions were routine at Danforth, where evangelistic zeal ran high!) My dad, always up for a challenge, encouraged me to invite my entire class, and said that he would rent a bus for the occasion.

The prize was a free week at Elim Camp in Beaverton, Ontario, on Lake Simcoe. Apparently, there was no money to send me to camp but there were funds to rent a bus. Go figure. By the way, this is *not* a memory in retrospect that I am proud of. But it was fun and humorous—if not very grandiose of my father.

Indeed a bus was needed to transport my class of thirty kids to Danforth, a good half an hour away by car from our school community. The bus was rented as promised, and I and thirty of my closest friends traipsed down the aisle for the opening Sunday school time.

There were little gasps as one after another, we all marched, single file, down the aisle, led by yours truly. I won the contest, but I confess that this wasn't the most effective evangelism method—another example of misplaced zeal, but one which still was fun for us all. None of my classmates continued to come to Sunday school with me, as the bus service was a one-time thing only.

Incidentally, during my winning week at Elim Camp, I won the competition for who could eat the most Parsley. And I haven't cared for it since! Apparently contests of every kind—including the herb-eating variety—were in vogue during the late fifties in Toronto's Christian circles. I guess I must have enjoyed competitions.

Music was woven into my church life just as it was my home and school life. As soon as I was old enough, probably about 16 or 17, I played the piano for church services. I learned to play by ear from my mother and a church lady named Lynn Reid.

Singing in the choir and performing solos were also an important part of my training. I sang my first solo in front of church when I was about seventeen.

"I'll be a friend of his through all my days,
I'll walk life's road with him and sing his praise ..."

(The song is titled "I'll Be a Friend of His," and I recently sang it at a "Tell My Story" presentation at Breton Woods, a retirement community where I now live.)

At one point, I joined the choir in singing during a missionary conference at church. From my spot in the choir loft, I was struck by a wall hanging by the front of the church, with a picture of planet earth and the following words:

"The field is the world."

I can still see the banner in my mind's eye, clear as day. That has been my calling and I have never forgotten it. Little did I know then that I would go on to travel the world and find another part of my field of ministry, yes, around the world. Thank you Lord Jesus for that prophetic symbol which has come to pass in my life over and over again. Another *miracle*?

***

Looking back, I know I was blessed with the family God gave me. After my mother's conversion, she was a changed person. She was more loving, patient, and healthier too. She definitely interceded for her family consistently and prayer was a big part of her life.

I usually called her with our family's prayer requests: travel, camps, exams, etc. and I knew she would be praying. Yes, we experienced much chaos, and challenges paying the bills because of my dad's inability to be organized in his business. We experienced much anxiety in the sometimes-abusive atmosphere emanating from their fighting.

But in spite of all of that negativity, we were loved dearly, and we always had lots of good food to eat, music to make, and fun to experience. Most important of all, after my mother and I became believers, we had Christ in our home. Salvation, of course, is the most important *miracle*, one that endures through eternity.

I continue to give thanks for faithful servants such as Billy Graham, who obeyed God's call on his life to preach the Gospel to his "field." I was just one person in that bountiful harvest. And dear George and Flo—what an example they are of listening to the Holy Spirit and following his leading!

Because they obeyed a divine prompt to do something peculiar and attend a church they had never set foot in, my whole family was changed for the better, not just in my generation but hopefully for the generations to come. As a result of the miracle of salvation in our family, I will be reunited with my parents and siblings, joined together to praise God forever around his majestic throne.

Musing

I'm so glad that Jesus is my Savior, my *miracle*. Just as the Scripture says, as I've trusted in him, He has directed my path. I continue to ask him to help me to trust him more and more.

> For God so loved the world that He gave His only begotten Son that whoever believes on Him will not perish but have everlasting life (John 3:16).

Know Jesus, call on him, trust in him, and He will direct your path.

Chapter 3

My Education

Seek ye first the kingdom of God and His righteousness. And all these things shall be added unto you (Matthew 6:33).

In Grade Nine, I made the transition from Bedford Park School to Lawrence Park Collegiate. My older siblings had gone there, and in fact, Bruce was still a popular upperclassman when his little sister showed up, eager and naïve as to what this high school business entailed.

My girlfriends and I walked to school, lugging our heavy book bags the mile or so up Lawrence Avenue to get to our destination. Sometimes, depending on the weather, we'd take the bus or get a ride.

I did end up getting my driver's license at age sixteen—and occasionally my dad would allow me to drive the Ford station wagon to school when I was in Grade Thirteen, which at that time was the completion of high school and entrance requirements for University. The Ontario education system had five years of secondary in those days.

Like every high school student, I had to find my place in the halls. Where would I fit in? What kinds of things could I do? I was pretty sure sports were now in my rearview mirror, although I did swim on the synchronized swim team.

I also tried out to be a cheerleader at Bruce's urging. He was popular and had lots of friends; he wanted his sister to be "important" as well. There was only one spot for a Grade Nine girl on the cheer team, but I tried out anyway, knowing that Bruce had made his buddies vote for me.

Alas, their efforts were in vain because another girl was chosen. I was so disappointed I never tried out again, although I can understand why I was not chosen as sports have never been my forte. In fact, the truth be known—and my family will vouch for this—I've always been a little awkward in the athletic department.

Cheer was not for me, but I dabbled in other things like being an editor of *The Robour*, our school yearbook. Mainly I found a place to belong in three familiar domains: my faith, academics, and music— always music. That first year of school, I joined the Inter School Christian Fellowship (ISCF). We held Bible studies and ski weekends and could invite our friends as an outreach event.

A highlight of my time at Lawrence Park was undoubtedly being chosen among the student body to interview famous Canadian author Morley Callaghan on a television program. Best known for his novels such as *My Beloved* and *More Joy in Heaven*, Callaghan also wrote short stories and plays.

As a great book lover, this was a thrill indeed. I was in Grade Eleven or Twelve, and by then we had a TV. Our family and some of my friends excitedly gathered around the twin stereo/ television set to watch the interview.

***

I've always loved reading. We weren't allowed to read at the dinner table but sometimes, not able to resist the temptation to read what was happening in my Nancy Drew mystery, I would try to hide the book on my knees under the table cloth as I concentrated on "looking down at my plate."

Oh, oh. My mother soon caught on to what I was doing. Fast forward to today: I should be understanding of the "no cell phones" edict at the dinner table, as I've often seen that same behavior with cell phones and the snap chatting that *must* continue.

Studying was also a huge part of my teen years. Looking back, I think I was driven. I just *had* to achieve. I think it was one way to overcome the anxiety at home. In later years I've realized the motivation for this drive and have come to terms with it. My identity as an unconditionally loved child of God does *not* depend on my achievements.

At home on Wanless Avenue, quiet was in short supply so I would plug in my hair dryer (*sans* bonnet) to create a cone of white noise. It's funny how now one can buy a white noise machine or download a white noise app. My inventor dad and I could have made a bundle if we had thought of this idea back in 1960!

I would pore over my books and notes every day, hair dryer blaring its static surround sound. My mother would bring me up a bowl of hot, buttered popcorn to my room as I studied. No one in my family had been to university, so she had her hopes set on me. In her mind, popcorn might enable me on my academic path.

Sometimes boys from school came over and joined me in munching popcorn as we quizzed each other for a test. We'd sit around the table doing homework. There's still nothing better than a bowl of popcorn in the evenings, studying or no studying.

I must have been a little dense when it came to romance at that point. I never picked up the message that they were over because they wanted to go out with me. Or maybe in retrospect it was fear covered by denial. At a high-school reunion thirty-years after those study interludes, a gentleman told me how he had been one of those boys, hitting the books with me on Wanless Avenue.

"You told me that I was a great guy," he said, "and that if you were to be dating, which you weren't, you would be happy to date me. I left your house feeling good about myself and not rejected, even though you had turned me down." Apparently, I had let him down easy, refusing his offer of a date in a tactful way.

I was too busy with music to bother much with boys. I'm amazed now I even had time to study or do anything extra at all. I played the violin in Mrs. Kusmick's orchestra, participated in the *National Youth Orchestra* one summer, played piano, and sang in the choir and as a soloist in church.

I also practiced four to five hours a day for my ARCT (Associate of the Royal Conservatory of Toronto, a certificate program that encompasses all levels and spans eleven grades from beginner to certification as an ARCT and a solo performer).

Looking back, it was certainly a crazy schedule, and I can't imagine ever expecting my child or grandchild to live such a schedule. It was driven. The upside: music for me was always relaxing. Believe it or not, I loved practicing the piano. I could get lost in my music, even in the scales. The rhythm and repetition was calming.

To get that much practice in, I had to do at least an hour of scales, early in the morning, much to the annoyance of my brother, Bruce, who would sleepily bang on the floor below him with a broom stick to get me to knock it off. Sometimes my musical interests and commitments would clash.

For example, in Grade Thirteen, Mrs. Kuzmick's orchestra, was to take a road trip from Toronto to Ottawa for a concert. Since I was practicing so much a day for my ARCT (the second time around), I didn't think I had time for a road trip, so my dad bought me an airplane ticket for my very first flight. Yes, sometimes he spoiled me.

I wonder what all of the other kids in the orchestra thought of that special treatment? It does seem "over the top," but nobody said anything. Apparently back then I didn't have the ability to say "No" to activities.

When I was sixteen in Grade Twelve, I tried for the ARTC, the highest piano performance exam offered. Why did I do this? In retrospect I don't know, as I did fail it the first time and was utterly devastated. The examiners said that I didn't yet have the maturity in my music, although the technique was good. Duh. I was so young and under so much pressure.

The following year after Grade thirteen, I tried it again and did pass, thankfully, but it hadn't been easy to spend another entire year practicing scales and Liszt, Chopin, Schumann, and Beethoven for hours on end. The investment of time was staggering, really.

Looking back at all those commitments now, it seems way over the top and a bit ridiculous. At the time I must have thought it was all worth it. Anyway, on the upside, music was my joyful place, and kept me sane and focused.

Grade Thirteen gave me a chance to develop as a person and get a little older before university, although I was still very young and naïve. God was growing me, from a barely teen who thought for a moment she might want to become a cheerleader to an eighteen-year-old who thought she wanted to be a doctor. However, I still had some detours to take before I would wind up on the clear path of my adulthood.

I studied long hours to try and get into medical school. In those days, women seeking to work at the top of the medical field faced an uphill battle. This was 1962, and even seven years later in 1969, women only comprised 9% of medical students in American medical schools.

At that time, female students were required to have much higher grades than their male counterparts. The reasoning being, we learned from the dean of medicine, was that women who completed medical school would inevitably get married, have children, and drop out of the profession, wasting their medical training.

Some would call this a systematic exclusion of women from medical schools. It was definitely a sign of the times, because today there are more women than men enrolled in medical schools in North America.

Nonetheless, I studied diligently and was given a provisional acceptance to the University of Toronto's medical school at Christmas, midway through grade 13, a victory for me, and my family rejoiced. However, when I received my June Ontario exam results, my grades were just beneath the level that would have allowed me to enter medical school.

Upon my rejection to pre-meds, my brother Bruce marched me down to the dean's office to lobby for me—to no avail. I was so discouraged and upset.

Two failures: a failure to pass my ARTC in grade 12 and a failure to go to medical school in grade 13. Yes, sometimes failure is an important part of our growth as individuals. However, that was a huge blow to my self-esteem and confidence as a yet undifferentiated, struggling teenager.

Why didn't I realize at the time that I was way too busy and had pushed myself to the limit, and probably over the limit? As I look back at that time, I must have been totally stressed out.

The dean however, recommended a slightly different route, one that would still get me into medical school if I worked hard enough. It was a track called Biological and Medical Sciences and included all the pre-meds and first year medical school courses.

Upon completion, those of us on this track were guaranteed a place to complete the other three years of medical school to become a doctor. Ironically, this was a more robust course, but I guess there were more openings available.

University of Toronto

In the fall of 1962, I entered the University of Toronto as an Honors Science major. This course included 4 years of Physics, Chemistry, Anatomy, Microbiology, Calculus, Statistics, Embryology, Physical Chemistry, and all subjects that would be helpful for a medical researcher, since an extra year of science and mathematics enhanced the pre-med experience.

I managed to pass (thankful for the "bell curve") and could have completed the rest of medical school. However, God had different plans for me (more on that later).

Looking back, I'm wondering what value it was for me to work so hard on subjects that I would never use. I found the subjects interesting, but ask me detailed questions about any of that subject material and I would be at a loss.

Hopefully, it helped me to train my brain. I do enjoy praying for people who need healing, as I can picture the human anatomy that I learned. And I also am quite intrigued with neuroanatomy.

In recent years, I've published some original research on spiritual interventions in psychotherapy, so those years of difficult study did help me. Who would have thought? I guess it does help to write one's memoir and to know that God doesn't waste any experience to help us grow.

I would have preferred to live in residence, but I was paying my own way and could not afford to swing room and board along with the $400 in tuition, which I earned at my summer job. What a difference from today! My hair dryer/white noise machine graduated from high school and served me throughout university, as I lived at home. It solved the problem of how to concentrate in a noisy, busy household.

Faith was still a core part of my life. I continued to attend Danforth Gospel Temple and attended a Sunday school class for college students taught by Pastor Faught. While many fundamental Bible churches were discouraging their young people from higher education, Dr. Faught strongly encouraged us in our studies.

In class we explored the difficult faith questions that arise among college-aged people, coming of age in a world that could be hostile. Dr. Faught encouraged us to grapple with our doubts, not deny them. "Bring them to God in honesty, because you all have to own your own personal faith," he would tell us, "God doesn't have grandchildren."

This mindset was hugely helpful to me in my leadership role with Intervarsity as I learned how to be a more effective envoy for Christ, holding prayer meetings in the dorms and witnessing to my unchurched friends. At one point, the Christians on campus challenged the atheists to a debate.

The president of the atheists group became a Christian afterwards and later went on to become an Anglican priest. Assuredly, God was moving through the campus at the University of Toronto, and it was wonderfully affirming to be part of his work there.

As usual, books came before boys, even though I was a grownup and a university student. In my first year of university, I did go on a few dates, but deep down I felt as though I would never find someone to love me and marry me. I don't really know why except dating was still an unknown and I didn't have much confidence in myself.

However, little did I know there was someone out there, someone more perfectly imperfect for perfectly imperfect me.

Musing

Although failures for me were difficult at the time, to say the least, in retrospect I can see how God helped me through them and brought good for me out of the disappointments. I had to give them over to God.

What failures have you experienced?

Chapter 4

Tuesday at Five

Delight yourself in the Lord and He will give you the desires of your heart (Psalm 37:4).

At the beginning of my second year, I was scouting around for some second-hand medical textbooks, which were costly brand new. While attending a Bible study with a group from the Faculty of Medicine, I met a guy named Alvin Kelly who was a medical student and asked him if he happened to be selling any medical books.

"No," he said, "but my friend, Steve, might have some." Alvin introduced me to Steve King, a tall, dark, and handsome blue-eyed medical student who indeed had the exact textbooks I was looking for.

"Why don't you meet me at the hospital cafeteria where I work, (he was doing a three-month stint at Toronto General), and I can give you the books there," Steve suggested.

The next day I realized that I had a physical chemistry class at noon, which would present a conflict for meeting this Steve King person in the cafeteria. I discussed the dilemma with my lab partner, David, and he encouraged me to go. "I'll take notes for you," he said. "Go."

Amazing how a simple decision can change the course of one's life. I went to the hospital cafeteria with no expectation except to pay Steve for the books and eat my sack lunch brought from home.

My mother loved to bake and was a gifted cook as I've said before—everything was homemade. She made my lunch every day during university, and sometimes she made my favorite meatloaf sandwiches on homemade buns. (When we ate during a noon lecture, my classmates would get a whiff of my incredible-smelling lunch and would roll their eyes in jealousy, which never induced me to share.) I guess I was spoiled in that way. She was so excited that I was going to university that she wanted to do anything to help.

Upon arrival in the hospital cafeteria, Steve motioned for me to line up for the food line. I suddenly realized that we were going to eat lunch together although the word "date" hadn't been mentioned. When I offered to pay for my lunch, he insisted that he would pay. I discreetly dropped my sack lunch in the trash and sat down across from Steve at one of the cafeteria tables.

Steve's friends seemed to know exactly what kind of meeting this was, as one by one they marched by our table greeting Steve with none-too-subtle smirks on their faces. Pretending I didn't catch on to their shenanigans was difficult as I tried to hide my emotions and embarrassment.

Oh, my goodness. All at once I was so nervous I could hardly eat what was on my plate. Don't ask me what it was! As Steve and I chatted, sharing dreams and faith issues and getting-to-know-you talk, I strategically moved my fork around the plate, lifting it at socially suitable intervals to my mouth.

Steve must have thought that I had a very birdlike appetite (he was to be in for a big surprise). I mentioned to Steve that on the upcoming weekend I would be attending our Intervarsity Christian Fellowship (IVCF) retreat up north in Muskoka cottage country at the ministry's Campus in the Woods.

"Oh, I'm planning on going out of town with some buddies to a football game this weekend," he said, nonchalantly.

Three days later, after classes I was dragging my books, sleeping bag, and a small suitcase across Queens Park to meet the bus for the trip north. Guess who showed up in the middle of the park to help me carry my stuff? Steve walked my belongings and me to the bus and waved me off.

"Have a good time," he said. I smiled and waved back. My, he did have the bluest eyes.

The next day, I sat in an amphitheater of logs in the woods, listening to a message given by a former NFL football player. My eyes took in the vista of a gorgeous blue, calm lake surrounded by the reds, oranges, bronzes, and yellows of the exquisite Ontario autumn foliage.

I was moved by the football player's inspirational words. *I wish Steve King had come so he could hear this guy speak*, I mused. The thought surprised me. Why should I care if Steve King heard this message? I just met the guy.

After the service concluded, I turned around and looked up. There stood Steve at the top of the hill. Stone faced, I jerked my head back around and leaned in to my friend, Carole, sitting next to me, "He's here!"

She didn't even have to ask who *he* was. I had mentioned his name to Carole already, asking her if she knew him. I experienced a jolt of jumbled emotions: happiness, shock, and fright! Overall, though, it was a lovely surprise.

Later as we were both clearing up in the dining hall after lunch, I ran into him.

"Oh, you came," I said coolly.

"Hi," he responded, with equal cool.

A deep conversation, I must say.

***

My chance to get to know this man on a deeper level came quickly. Later on that same Sunday afternoon, I held a meeting as chairman of our missions committee. Steve joined us.

I handed out questionnaires to the group but had to leave early to get back to Toronto for a concert date at Hart House. "I'll collect the completed questionnaires and bring them to you tomorrow at the Medical Building," Steve offered, quite graciously, I thought.

I was in the middle of an anatomy lab with my three fellow lab partners, working on our cadaver when Steve arrived. (We called the cadaver "Ernest" since we could say we were working in dead earnest. Okay, you don't have to laugh, but I thought it was funny!) Steve pulled up his sleeves and dug in—literally—helping us with our difficult dissection project. After all, he was an experienced medical student and had taken the course already.

It was a beautiful fall day, and the sun was shining through the lab window, highlighting Steve in all his cadaver-dissecting glory. I wasn't really looking at the cadaver, as his gorgeous blue eyes mesmerized me. I don't think I learned much anatomy that day.

Steve stayed for the rest of the lab and walked me to the trolley on Bloor Street, which would take me to the subway, and then the bus home. "Can I call you?" Steve asked me just as the trolley door was closing. I think I nodded but didn't have a chance to give him my phone number, but my heart was fluttering.

He found it and gave me a call, inviting me to a home football game at Varsity Stadium. It was our first official date.

All the females in my family were in a state of excitement, especially me. I tried on several outfits and asked for the discerning feedback of my mother and sisters. I remember exactly what I wore: a brown jersey skirt and top, a camel hair coat, and little brown pumps.

Steve came to pick me up by trolley, subway, bus, and walking. I don't remember who won the game, but I do remember enjoying his company, even though I was a little nervous. We returned from the game by the same trolley, subway, and bus to my home.

That same evening, Steve had planned to move from his parents' home to a flat downtown on College Street, close to the university. I saw my brother's red convertible parked in front of our house and offered to at least drive Steve to the subway to save him some time. Bruce, who was six years older than me, allowed me to drive his car sometimes, and I knew where the key was hidden. We hopped into the car and I attempted to show off, anxiously gunning the gas as we cruised around the corner.

It was less impressive when we were immediately stopped by a police officer on Lawrence Avenue for speeding. My face turned bright pink as I ruefully accepted my first ticket for a whopping $70, a budget buster considering my tight finances. Steve offered to pay half of the ticket, which struck me as gentlemanly indeed. I graciously accepted. *Oh, maybe I should hold onto this guy*, I thought.

"And here I thought you were slow," he teased me. Well, he had to find out about me some time.

***

We fell into a pleasant routine of dating for the next year. On Wednesday nights at 10 p.m., we had a standing phone date (much like the "Tuesday at five" dates we would have later). Every Saturday night, we had an established date where we would go to the movies, or to the theater, concerts, skating, walking, and eating.

We could get a steak dinner at *Steak n More* for $1.99, which was a great deal since it included steak, baked potato, salad, a drink, and strawberry shortcake. We often ate there and then walked around downtown Toronto—a cheap but lovely date.

Sometimes, on a Thursday night Steve would make tea biscuits at his flat and bring them, complete with jam and tea, over to where I was studying in the university library. Then he would walk me to the bus stop. He would send me these great cards in the mail, sometimes once a week, some of which I still have. Amid the constant "crunch time" of intense studying, I soaked up Steve's thoughtfulness and kindness.

At Christmas that year, he invited me over to meet his stoic English family, who struck me as extremely quiet and mannerly compared to my raucous Irish clan. During the meal, I was so impressed that no one shouted over anyone else and we were all given time to finish our sentences. I found out later from his sister, Lynn, that I had been the first girl Steve had ever brought home. *It must be serious*, she thought.

We continued dating, although the "m" word never came up unless we were dismissing it. "I don't think I will get married since I am going to be a missionary doctor," I would say, casually.

"Oh, I don't plan to get married either," he said, nonchalantly. And so it went, until a bit later in the story. I think those proclamations made us much more relaxed and we could just enjoy getting to know one another without pressure.

After a while, he kissed me for the first time on the doorstep of 212 Wanless Avenue. I saw stars and walked into my home woozy with feeling. I don't remember if one heel came off the ground or not.

"What happened to you?" My sister asked, smirking. Apparently, I wore my heart on my sleeve (or my face) even back then. My children tell me I still do. Though marriage was supposedly off the table, it was really on the table and everybody suspected it. Or at least everybody knew it was a possibility. They'd never seen me like this before, all googly eyed.

"How do you know if you're in love?" I posed this question to my sister-in-law, as she was drying the dishes one day in the kitchen at home.

"One way to tell," she said, "is to try to imagine your future without that person in it. If you can't, it's probably love."

I stubbornly clung to my independent ideals, but I could not imagine a future without Steve King. "I think I'm in love," I said, as my heart did flip-flops.

That feeling was about to be confirmed when Steve took off for a four-month stint in the Canadian arctic, working a good-paying summer job to help pay for medical school. It was the summer of 1963, and I was sad at the thought of our separation. I wasn't looking forward to being without the company of this guy who had become so important to me.

Before Steve left, he gave me a piece of paper with a verse written on it:

I have set the Lord always before me: because He is at my right hand I shall not be moved. Therefore, my body shall rest in peace (Psalm 16:8).

I keep that piece of paper in my treasure box. Many years later, after Steve's death, I read that verse in his handwriting for the umpteenth time and was inspired to write a song called "His Love Endures Forever." I finish this memoir with the words to this song. I knew well that my strength and emotional support came from God alone, yet I missed Steve.

This verse was and is such a comfort to me. Steve and I had grown spiritually together during that first year of dating. I knew his spirit and heart were surrendered to God. We prayed that our relationship would be surrendered, as well.

We said goodbye that summer of 1963, and a piece of my heart flew off to Eureka, in Canada's untamed Northwest Territories. Steve would be working for the Department of Transport in a joint communication and weather station project conducted by both Canada and the U.S. from mid-May to September.

His home for those months was three hundred miles south of the North Pole on Ellesmere Island in the Qikiqtaaluk Region of the arctic-archipelago (now part of the Canadian territory of Nunavut).

In 1963, there was no such thing as the Internet or cell phones. Literally, this place was unreachable by your basic landline telephone! The only way we could hear one another's voices was by ham radio.

Every Tuesday at five p.m. I would rush home from my job at the oil company and wait breathlessly for my telephone to ring. Steve would send a ham radio message to Ray in Toronto, who had a phone patch, which hooked up his ham radio to a phone. The entire conversation was punctuated by Ray's interruptions of "over and out, over and out."

Ray was the silent listener to all our chats. He played a role in our courtship, and when Steve returned to Toronto we took him out for a meal and gave him Tim Horton's gift cards and a piece of Arctic soapstone.

Piles and piles of letters were sent back and forth from sizzling hot Toronto to chilly Ellesmere Island. The mail service was dependent on whether a transport plane happened to fly into Steve's outpost with supplies. Oh, how I looked forward to those letters!

Steve would usually write something every day until the plane came in so sometimes the letters would be ten to fifteen pages long, written in his small handwriting. At times there would be photos of Eureka tucked inside, a visual peek at his far away life.

He also wrote and compiled a booklet of poetry, filled with these amazing poems about love, prayer, and about our experiences from the past year. Here's a snippet from one such poem:

"Love is an artery between two glad hearts

With each of the lovers supplying the parts.

The compassionate flow from one to the other

Can never be lessened by age or another."

How I wish now that I could have given him one of my healthy arteries for his heart so that he would still be with me. Sad, sad, sad.

He wrote another poem entitled, "Absence makes the heart grow fonder." In it he described our time from the past year together. It was fifteen verses of rhyme describing some of our dates: "The Sound of

Music," "Tom Jones," Swiss Chalet, ice fishing, canoeing on Moon River, the Messiah at Christmas time, and the Missionary Committee where "we sort of formed a cooperative leadership, with God, and me, and you."

"Absence makes the heart grow fonder,

These words are true, believe, and hear;

God's plans for us will unfold wisely,

I love you, love you, Judy dear."

Steve could be so romantic, and he was truly a fine writer. Me? I would rather talk than write most of the time. That summer, though, I wrote my heart out, expressing myself in long, rambling letters.

At Steve's request, I even wrote newsy missives to a friend of his who never received any letters. Gary always returned them. He had someone to write to. Steve could be very sensitive to the needs of others.

It was a long, hot summer in Toronto, as part of my heart was in the arctic. Even as I played the song "From Greenland's Icy Mountains" at Friday night youth group meetings, I instantly connected it with my man in an icy locale. Steve was never far from my thoughts.

***

In the fall, when Steve returned from his arctic depot to Toronto, we continued our once-a-week phone calls and date nights. The tea biscuits in the library on Thursday nights and $1.99 dinners at *Steak and More* on Saturday nights continued.

But Steve was scared. He asked for a break in November of that year, a break that ended up lasting two weeks. I was confused and unhappy. I didn't know what to do, since I didn't want to break up.

I ended up going to the store, bought some wool, a pattern and some knitting needles and started knitting Steve a pair of slippers for Christmas. Denial? Crazy? Yes. (However, those navy, nubby slippers lasted for decades.)

I waited, knitted, and prayed. Of course, I had studying (a lot of it) to do as well. His roommate told me to let him go but I couldn't seem to do that. He called up after two weeks and asked me for another date, saying that he missed me. Did I miss him too?

We were back on as a couple. From that point on, we considered marriage as a probable outcome, though we were totally absorbed in studying for our difficult courses at the university.

Over Christmas, we both attended the Inter Varsity Missions Conference in Urbana, Illinois, with our friends Alvin and Maureen. Billy Graham was the speaker on New Year's Eve, and I was moved again to hand over every part of my life, including my relationship with Steve.

When that next summer came around, Steve and a buddy, Dyson, took a trip to B.C. in his friend's Volkswagen. He was gone for a few weeks, but it was nothing compared to the previous summer's four and a half months in the Arctic. Still, my heart was knit with his by then, and I missed him on a deeper, more elemental level.

We had conversations about marriage from time to time, but hadn't committed to any plans. Marriage is a life-changing decision, and it was too scary still for both of us. Back then, we didn't read any books on marriage, delve into our pasts, do premarital counseling, or even talk much about emotions—unlike today where the opposite is true. I wish we had, because it would have been helpful.

As a young couple we had to stumble through issues of communication, emotions (or lack of them), finances, children etc., sometimes finding answers and sometimes not. We didn't understand then how different and opposite were our personalities. Often I've found that opposites do attract. Subconsciously we are looking to the other to fill in those parts of us that we don't have, and that was true of us.

When he came back from the trip, he surprised me at the door. I had stayed home sick from a church youth retreat, and was sporting a runny nose, red, puffy eyes, and unwashed hair. Right before he showed up, I had been bored and in the middle of experimenting with different shades of eye shadow. Honestly, I looked ridiculous and unkempt.

My ensemble of a wrinkly, shabby old top and shorts added to my overall pathetic appearance. My parents were out grocery shopping when Steve turned up at the door, so we were alone in the house. In walks Prince Charming, fresh off weeks of travel with a big agenda on his mind, only to be greeted by a sniffling, apprehensive girlfriend.

Ah, well, he had made up his mind to pop the question right there in my living room and I said yes, but it still took me by surprise. It was not like on TV or the movies. It was not a romantic proposal or atmosphere. Steve slid the ring in his pocket on my finger, but unfortunately it would only fit on my pinkie and would have to be resized.

My parents came home, laden with groceries, to the news of our engagement. Steve hadn't talked to my parents beforehand, as I wished he would have. I really recommend for that to happen.

I later wrestled with the Lord in prayer: "I love Steve, but I would be willing to give him up if that is what you are directing." I wanted to be sure that this was God's plan and not just mine. I can't emphasize how important this is: surrender it all to God. It's like an anchor and when you have stormy times later, you have a touchstone to which to go back.

"Did you get that ring out of the popcorn box?" My mom asked, squinting at my ring. Way to be excited, mother. Though, when you consider the awkwardness of the scene, with me sick and the ring on my pinkie finger, I can kind of understand her reaction. Kind of. After all, we had not mentioned the idea of marriage.

By the way, that sweet little diamond that he bought for me on a medical student's savings has increasing value to me today. I've had that little diamond and Steve's and my wedding bands made into a lovely ring which I proudly wear today.

I knew my mother truly loved Steve and had encouraged our courtship. One Sunday evening, before we were engaged, Steve was coming over, so she suggested I get all dressed up in one of her vintage evening gowns to surprise him. We ran around the house lighting candles everywhere and she marched my dad upstairs to his bedroom, clearing the living room for our romantic "visit."

She was just as excited as I was, as we peeked out the window watching for him to come down the street. The second he arrived she beat a hasty departure up to the bedroom. Part of the reason she made my dad go upstairs was because my dad really liked Steve and would sometimes monopolize our visits at my house.

He would wait up for us to return from a date and my dad would offer to make Steve a cup of tea or a steak sandwich or whatever Steve wanted, even a whole steak dinner if he had wanted it. My dad enjoyed his chats with Steve and food was a love language in the Briggs family. By now thus far, I'm sure you've noticed the mention of food.

Back to my engagement, I had to fully forgive my mother for her insensitive comments at such a tender and memorable moment in my life. *Thank you, Lord, for helping me forgive past hurts, big and small.* Even though I understood her reaction and let it go, I had to later do the forgiveness work. Understanding is not necessarily forgiveness.

All in all, my mother always wanted the best for me, and she loved me in so many other ways and looking back, I am very grateful for her love.

By then I was on track to enter my second year of medical school, after the four years of undergraduate studies which included pre-meds plus all of first year medical school. Back then, medical school consisted of two years of pre-meds and four years of medical school.

Steve and I had a long and serious conversation about our goals and plans. He said he wouldn't marry me if I went to medical school. It may sound sexist from our modern point of view, which I think it was, but his stance was in keeping with the conventional wisdom of the day. It was an exception and usually out of necessity if a mother with children worked outside of the home in those days.

Steve had decided, and I didn't have the courage, the insight, or the maturity to say, "Here's your hat, don't hurry!" But I was in love and just wanted to be with him.

Laying aside my dreams of being a doctor was not easy. It took me many years to come to terms with the choice I had made, a decision to acquiesce and turn my back on medical school. However, God is faithful. A year later, Steve changed his mind and said that he would support me if I still wanted to finish my medical training.

Who knows what that would have looked like or how it would have impacted our lives if I had done that? We'll never know. However, I continued to still look at that option throughout the years, even when we moved to Grand Rapids.

Fast forward at this writing: with further reflection on that subject, I came to understand that God had used Steve in that decision. Why really did I want to go into medicine and be a doctor? And why a doctor?

It recently occurred to me that I was trying to fulfill the words of my mother who often said my father was so smart that he should have been a doctor. I always wanted to please my mother and somehow make up for her the disappointments of her marriage and my father's choice of career.

In looking back at what doctors do—diagnose and prescribe with a limited time frame, with a need for a capacity to be a detailed person, sometimes with life and death hanging in the balance—I don't now believe that was the best option for me. God intervened, as I had asked him to many times.

My life verse is: "Trust in the Lord with all your heart and lean not on your own understanding. In all your ways acknowledge Him and He will direct your paths." I was doing my best to trust in him and He did direct my path, even when my trust was insufficient so many times in spite of myself.

So thank you, dear God, for leading me back then and thank you, Steve, for being "God with skin on" in my making that decision. I have some regrets that, over the years when I revisited the subject of medical school failure, I wasn't as clear about trusting God and Steve in that area.

God led me in another direction later, when my children were in high school and I decided to go to graduate school for my Masters of Social Work degree. Very clearly, this was the work which I was meant to do at this stage of our family life. I really enjoyed working as a mental health practitioner.

Presently, 2020, I love my work as a Christ-centered mental health professional in private practice, and I really wouldn't want to be doing anything else. I guess you could say, I became a doctor of the soul.

This profession has opened so many doors for me around the world. I love teaching and writing about the integration of the gospel, Biblical principles, and good mental health. And I love being a part of seeing God's healing power in setting the captives free.

Musing

I'm so glad that God led me, in spite of myself and my lack of trust.

Chapter 5

The Wedding

Hymn: *Praise My Soul the King of Heaven*
by Henry Fancis Lyute (1834)

Praise, my soul, the King of heaven;
To his feet your tribute bring.
Ransomed, healed, restored, forgiven,
Evermore his praises sing.
Alleluia, alleluia!
Praise the everlasting King

We set a wedding date for June 11, 1966, one week after I graduated with an Honor Bachelor of Science Degree and four days before Steve graduated with his M.D. (Medical Doctor) degree. Planning a wedding in the middle of extreme studying for physical chemistry, calculus, physics, and microbiology exams was stressful and, looking back, completely crazy.

In retrospect, my mother was right: it would have been a lot easier to listen to her and have the wedding at the end of the summer. But I was eager to leave home and I didn't want to be away from Steve since he was moving across Canada to Vancouver Island. Sorry, Mom!

Ever the list maker, I made lists and lists of my lists while trying to organize and pay for the wedding. As for paying, I wasn't sure how that was going to happen, but God provided in a surprising way.

My brother, Bruce, encouraged me to invest in penny stocks and one day I was waffling on the decision of whether to sell them or not. I don't remember why it was so urgent, but during a chemistry lab,

I ran back and forth to the pay phone (no cell phones then) consulting with Bruce. I finally decided to sell and my $400 turned into $800—enough to pay for my wedding.

There wasn't a risk involved here, because Bruce had promised me that $400 if it didn't work out. With borrowing a beautiful simple wedding dress and wearing the veil that my mother had worn, we were all set.

The afternoon reception was to be outdoors at the University of Toronto, in the quadrangle of Hart House. When my mother and I explored this as a venue, we came across a reproduction sculpture of Michelangelo's *David*, in all his naked glory.

My mother, who could be a bit Victorian in her ideas, asked the employee giving us a tour a question: "Will you be covering up that naked sculpture, or at least the part that shows the bare bottom and frontage?" she asked in all seriousness.

That story still makes me smile. And no, if you're wondering, for my reception David remained as he was, in all his naked glory. Nevertheless, this venue was ideal for a beautiful outdoor reception.

I'll never forget arriving to a flurry of the carillon bells from the bell tower. The bridesmaids all wore pink and carried bouquets of white and pink roses in full bloom. Oh, how fragrant they were! The pews of Danforth Gospel Temple were festooned with white satin ribbons with a rose and baby's breath intertwined through the bows.

My father and I rode together in a limousine to the church. I wanted a chariot, but they were literally all rented out. (This desire was rooted in my obsession with all things royal as I've mentioned before—and maybe a little grandiose of me. I am a lifelong fan of Queen Elizabeth.) A limousine would have to do.

Dad and I held hands the whole way from north Toronto to Danforth Gospel Temple in the east end, sweetly reminiscing the whole way. He was emotional and tender as we made that momentous journey to the church.

At the threshold of the sanctuary, I held my father's arm and waited for the entrance chord to introduce "Praise my Soul, the King of Heaven," grateful tears trickling down my face. Not too far though, because I didn't want to ruin my makeup. What a beautiful scene to behold with the cross as a centerpiece.

As I walked down that aisle, I smiled at everyone I loved, conscious of God's blessing in my life to be joined in marriage to that tall, handsome man, the love of my life. There was a trumpeter and an organist playing our favorite worship music. The lovely sounds fed my musical soul at one of the most crucial moments of my life.

After our wedding vows, Dr. Faught prayed for us: "Lord, may their life count for you." That was our desire as a couple and is still my desire today as I walk ahead as a single person without Steve.

In Canadian weddings there were typically lots of speeches and toasts. The best man, Alvin Kelly, who had introduced us, gave a toast to the bridesmaids, resplendent in their light pink gowns. Then my brother Bruce gave the toast to the bride, and as custom dictated, Steve as groom responded.

Dag recorded those speeches for us on a reel-to-reel tape. Later, he transferred them to ultra-modern cassettes, which were the latest thing at the time. Steve and I listened to them every year on our anniversary until he died. What a treasure to hear those beloved voices blessing us with their love! Those people are no longer with us, including Dag.

Dag was twenty years older than me, and Joyce twelve. I adored them both, and at times pretended this handsome young couple were my mom and dad. My mother was forty years old when I was born, and so my parents were much older.

As a twelve-year-old girl, I watched my sister and her husband closely as they grew together as a married couple. How they loved each other! Dag and Joyce were an early model for me of what marriage looked like, and now I was a married woman myself. The adventure had just begun.

Postscript: Our wedding bulletin included a poem Steve had written for the occasion.

Our Wedding Prayer

God, bless those who are gathered here today,
And other friends, who were unable to pass by this way,
Make this marriage service mean something close to each,
For we all have needs that You alone can reach.
God, bless Judy and me, especially at this important time,
Teach us from the start to place our hands in Thine.

Make us walk straightly, honestly, humbly, and yet sure,

Over life's tremulous pathways, in Your will remain secure.

God, bless the life together, that we begin this day,

The future is uncertain—help us always to pray,

Make us so truly thankful for our fortunate place,

Our home, families, church, and friends,

And most of all, Thy Grace.

Musing

I'm so thankful that we learned to trust God to lead us in finding the right partner for our lives. Knowing that we were in his will for our lives, helped us in times of trouble.

The Honeymooners

The two will become one flesh. So they are no longer two, but one flesh (Mark 10:8).

After every wedding comes a marriage, and ours began by driving across Canada, from Toronto to Victoria, British Columbia, where Steve would begin his medical internship. In today's terms, this would be about fifty hours in the car together, journeying about 4,000 miles.

On the way, as part of our honeymoon, we stayed in the famous Lake Louise/Banff area, in the mountains in a log cabin with a fireplace. Though it was a romantic setting, our experience was less than romantic. For one thing, I was exhausted from exams, graduating, getting married one week later, and attending Steve's graduation three days after our wedding.

I had left my home and family for the first time, and that was emotionally exhausting. To add to my troubles, I had never been in the mountains before and developed a bit of altitude sickness and probably an ear infection. Steve began our marriage by taking care of me lovingly, fetching me a hot water bottle from town and generally being loving to his new bride, who was not much company in her current state.

Thankfully, as I've said before, we had many wonderful, healthy "honeymoons" later throughout our life together, although the first one was a bit of a bust. Lately I've been hearing of couples settling into their new home first and resting before going on a honeymoon later; probably for some that's a good idea.

As we settled in to our first weeks and months of marriage in Victoria, I knew my mother had been right: postponing the wedding until the end of summer would have been prudent. Spent and homesick, the reality of life as a doctor's wife was beginning to dawn on me.

Steve was gone nearly all the time, fulfilling the demands of his internship. We flew home for our first Christmas, so that helped a little with the homesickness.

We newlyweds did have some lighter moments, though. Our apartment was right across from the hospital, so Steve could sneak home sometimes when he was on call. When a little kitten wandered in to the ER, Steve picked it up and brought it home for me. I'd grown up with my treasured cat, Twinkle, and Steve knew how much I liked cats, even though he didn't, or so he said.

History proved different. His bringing home Samantha (Sammy) made me feel cherished and understood. The next May, on Mother's Day, Steve placed a wrapped gift and Mother's Day card next to Sammy's food bowl. He got a lot of mileage out of that orphan kitten!

We lived at 850 Quadra, in the interns' apartment, which also housed six other married couples whose husbands had been recruited by Victoria General Hospital from the University of Toronto. The Catholic sisters who operated the hospital were very kind to us, baking us cookies and providing steak dinners once a week for the interns and their families.

Are you surprised that I always remember the food? We had lots of fun together as six couples, including going to auction sales to furnish our sparse apartments. My excitement at bargain hunting sometimes exceeded my common sense.

One time I got such a good deal on a vacuum I bought it even though we didn't have any carpets. Another time, I couldn't resist a large box of piano music, though we didn't have a piano—yet. I always joked that having a piano was written into my marriage vows! I didn't think I could exist without my piano.

Later, Steve and I traveled to Vancouver and spent time with Aunt

Mabel (my mother's sister) and Uncle Charlie. My uncle helped us find and buy an old upright piano, which we would end up hauling with us to the arctic. I've never been without a piano since.

***

My brother, Bruce, used to say to my mother, "You'd better teach that girl to cook. No man will ever want to marry her."

My dear mother had the best comeback: "I figure if she can read a book and do chemistry experiments, she'll be able to read a cook book."

Well, I knew how to make one thing—rhubarb pie, as I had made it with my mother on one occasion. However, man (and wife) cannot live on pies alone. Thankfully, Steve had been cooking for himself for a few years at his flat, which he and Alvin rented from "Captain Peter" downtown by the university.

During courtship days, he made me roast beef and Yorkshire pudding for dinner. The way to a woman's heart is through her stomach. Oh, oh. I think I have that expression backwards.

The first time as a married couple that we invited another couple for dinner I went into a big tizzy as I tried to "whip up" roast beef with Yorkshire pudding and strawberry shortcake with homemade tea biscuits for dessert. The menu was far beyond my skill level, yet Steve wasn't helping. Finally, when I was ready to explode, he came in to the kitchen to help me cook.

On St. Patrick's Day that first year, I served Steve all-green food all day: green scrambled eggs, green mashed potatoes, green milk, and every kind of green vegetable. It's amazing he stayed with me after that display of creativity, but he knew I was merely showing loyalty to the country in which my mother was born.

The next year, when we lived in Hazelton, B.C., I learned to bake bread, make pies for the freezer, and can tomatoes, fruit and pickles. When you're first married, you want to try everything just to prove that you can do it (then you can let it go, if it isn't a necessity). I even attempted to make green hotdog relish from cucumbers.

I kept adding more flour to the bubbling pot since it didn't seem to be thickening. Pretty soon the big, gooey, green mess boiled over the kettle onto the stove, and down to the floor. That canning project went to the trash. I decided to let go of most canning, though I continued to can my mother's wonderful chili sauce in the fall. It filled our various homes with a pungent aroma that always brings back warm memories.

Back in Victoria, learning to cook was fine and dandy, but I wanted to work. Armed with an honors science degree and a "Mrs." I felt I was now a woman of the world and would easily find suitable employment.

One morning, I got all dressed up in a black and white checkered skirt and jacket, with white gloves and a black and white hat and marched down to the glamorous Empress Hotel to apply for a job. Much to my dismay, this classy hotel turned me down. "You're over-qualified," they said, flatly.

Trudging home slowly and tearfully, I tried to make sense of this disappointing turn of events. Why, they wouldn't even hire me as a chambermaid and here I could have been in medical school!

This setback turned out to be a setup, as I was hired at Victoria General as an EKG technician (cardiograms). I was even on call some-times, a possibility I responded to by carefully placing each item of clothing out on the chair for quick and easy access, should I get called in the night. This cracked Steve up, especially since I never did get called.

As you've read by now, music was always a part of my life. That year I took violin lessons again and joined the Victoria Symphony Orchestra, which delighted me, especially since I was playing my father's antique violin. Between my work and Steve's internship, there wasn't much time left over, but we did find time for recreation in the stunning beauty of the Pacific Northwest.

On weekends we would take ferries over to the gulf islands for picnics and hikes. We camped together with other intern couples on Long Beach on the west coast of Vancouver Island, cooking our food over a campfire and excitedly collecting what we thought were clams. Our west coast friends laughingly informed us they were not clams but an inedible type of mussels. We camped down the coast of California, sleeping in our pup tent on the beach. Oh, those were the days!

Quite often we'd visit with my father's sister, my Aunt Evelyn (I am her namesake) and Uncle Rod who lived in Victoria. Being with Aunt Evelyn and Uncle Rod, who taught me to drive stick shift, helped alleviate my loneliness for home.

After my hospital job, I worked in the social work field doing foster home and adoption supervision which put me in good stead for my future, unbeknown to me at the time. The car that I had to use for this job was a VW Beetle stick shift, so thanks to my uncle for his help.

Musing

I loved being married. It's so great to have that one person who knows you better than anyone else and is always there for you. Now single, I sure miss the love of my life.

Chapter 6

First Nations Adventures

Jesus answered, "Everyone who drinks this water will be thirsty again, but whoever drinks the water I give him will never thirst. Indeed, the water I give him will become in him a spring of water welling up to eternal life" (John 4:13).

We survived our first year of marriage, which was a mix of fun adventures and the difficulty that comes from trying to meld two lives into one. I enjoyed being married and liked saying that I was "Dr. King's wife."

Steve kindly recognized my homesickness for my family in Toronto and surprised me with plane tickets to travel to Toronto for our first Christmas. The reunion was wonderfully nourishing to my soul as we had celebrations with both families.

Back in Victoria, we were thinking about our future after internship and talking about having children, fortunately, something that we both strongly desired. The next two years would be a fulfillment of that dream in Hazelton, the birthplace of David, and in Mission City, the birthplace of Deborah.

Not long after we returned to Victoria from Toronto, a doctor visited our Sunday school at the Baptist church where we attended and told us about a United Church Mission to the First Nations people in Hazelton, British Columbia.

Hazelton, located in northern British Columbia, was a village of about 300 people. As a teenager, I had been a counselor at a camp for Natives in Ontario and always had an affinity for this people group.

Steve and I got excited as we considered how this opportunity could be the fulfillment of our individual dreams to be medical missionaries. It also seemed like a good place to raise a family. Steve would work at the tiny United Church hospital, the only hospital for hundreds of miles in any direction, and I would work as a social worker for the Canadian Government.

As we researched Hazelton, we learned that our new home was the original gateway and staging area for the Omineca Gold Rush of 1869-73 and boasted the distinction of having dozens of howling sled dogs. Nearly everyone had their own team, and many dogs ran free. But before we made our final decision, Steve sat me down and told me something important:

As mentioned earlier, the idea of me finishing medical school was in the back of Steve's mind. We talked about that again before making our decision to move to Hazelton. "If you really want to go back to medical school, I will support you fully," he said.

I appreciated that but at that point had lost the desire for medical school and was happy to move on to a mission opportunity. Steve's words made me feel a sense of relief that now I was free to make that decision. However, we both knew we were meant to move to Hazelton for the next adventure and the next chapter of our lives.

***

We lived in Hazelton on a compound with the hospital, the chapel, the nurses' residence, and the other doctor's residence. The hospital was a two-story building and just looked like a big house to me. It had a simple lab, but no blood was available, so folks would have to be taken further north to Terrace, B.C., for blood.

The anesthesia at the Hazelton hospital was an ether mask administered by the doctor. Even in those days this was a little archaic. There was also an X-Ray machine and a primitive surgical suite. Steve had a three-minute walk down the path to work.

Our home was modern considering the backwoods locale: a two-story, three-bedroom, two-bathroom house. We planted grass in the yard and foraged in the local woods to dig up small evergreen trees to plant along a winding path to our house. I planted flowers and hung hanging baskets, which made everything pretty and homey.

By this time we had added a dog, a black lab called Spike, to keep company with our cat, Sammy, whom we had brought from Victoria. Somehow they defied the proverbial fighting metaphor, instead seeming to love each other as "cat and dog." They played and slept together and were the best of friends.

It was fun to watch them. If Spike saw another dog chasing Sam, he would chase the dog away, giving Sam time to climb a tree. On frosty winter nights we would find them sleeping together on their cozy rug, cuddled together against the cold.

One time, Spike got hurt and was stumbling along, in terrible pain. Steve took him to the X-ray machine at the hospital and took images of his spine and tail, late one night. Can you imagine the next day when the lab tech came in and looked at the X-ray? Was this a new variety of human with a tail? But it made for a good tale—ha!

During those years, our experiences living among Indigenous peoples were rich, fascinating, and heart expanding. My job with the Department of Northern Affairs as a social worker entailed working with three or four families and about twenty children among the First Nations peoples in our village.

We learned early on that it was crucial for us to adopt a posture of listening and learning about their culture and trying to fit in with them, as opposed to trying to fit them into our culture. As a government employee supporting these at-risk families, I raised awareness and funds to build them houses, held food drives, and taught them basic living skills. I felt it was critical to celebrate their culture and I encouraged parents to teach their children the native languages and creative arts.

One of my favorite projects was helping to build an art center with the goal of reclaiming the cultural creativity of the Kispiox and other tribes. Much of this had been lost, and it was pure joy to see them engaging in their ancient art forms such as intricate beadwork, ellipsoid shapes in their paintings, and totem poles.

At the invitation of Chief Edgar Good, we visited the Kispiox Indian village one afternoon. During the service, the chief issued an announcement: "Dr. King will now sing a solo." Well, Dr. King had never sung a solo in his life, so this came as a bit of a shock.

Steve leaned over to me. "They mean you," he whispered, somewhat urgently.

"No, they didn't say me; they said 'Dr. King,'" I whispered back. "You can do it. Get up and sing 'Just a Closer Walk with Thee.'" I knew Steve could pull that song off and he knew the guitar chords for it.

He had bought a guitar to relate to his Native male patients, because they always brought their guitars with them to the hospital. He would break the ice by asking them to show him some chords. Steve rose from his seat and embarked upon his short but sweet solo career, such as it was. It was a great hit with the crowd.

Another time we had gone to a wedding reception and we were the only white folk there. True to their custom the Native hosts invited the guests—us—to come to the platform and sing or speak. Instantly there was conflict between Steve and me as to what we would sing.

The year before at a church New Year's Eve party, Steve had strummed a ukulele and we had sung a crazy song:

We had some chickens, no eggs could they lay ... dah de dah.

One day a rooster flew over the yard.

They're laying eggs now, dah de dah,

Ever since that rooster flew over that yard.

We argued in whispers all the way up to the platform about what to sing. Steve wanted to sing the chicken song. I thought we should sing a hymn. After all, it was a wedding celebration. Steve won that round and we sang the chicken song while pretending to strum air ukuleles. The audience loved it, and I realized that my trying to spiritualize the experience had been silly. Sometimes, humor and lightheartedness win the day.

On another occasion, I was asked to play the pump organ for a Native wedding to be held in the Anglican Church. I arrived thirty minutes beforehand to play so there would be prelude music while folks came in. An hour later, with legs like rubber and my repertoire depleted, I was still playing that pump organ and only one person had arrived—just.

I learned that the Native culture was very organic, and a start time for anything was more of a suggestion than set in stone. This is true in other cultures and places such as West Africa I have experienced over the years. There's no right or wrong which often is dictated by the clock—just a different perspective on time compared to our Western, white mindset.

We would occasionally attend Native revival services that would sometimes last all night. We'd try to stay awake at least until midnight because that's when they took a break and served the food, and lots of it. During the services mothers would come up to Dr. King and ask him to look at their children for medical problems. Dr. King was popular at these gatherings.

We adored the indigenous children we got to know during our time there, becoming especially close to a few of them. I led a Canadian Girls in Training group once a week in one of the local villages and I taught piano lessons to some of the children. Their father would pay me with fresh caught Salmon speared from the Kispiox River or wild berries plucked from the woods.

***

Fresh off his one-year internship after medical school, Steve was green when he faced his first solo surgery. A family had been vacationing in the area, camping at a local campground, when their son began experiencing terrible abdominal pain.

They brought him in to the hospital where Steve worked, and he diagnosed the boy with a hot appendix. Dr. King had never taken out an appendix before, or anything else—at least not without supervision.

Steve called me in a panic. "Please pray, Jude," he begged me. "The boy's family is blindly trusting me." He couldn't believe that this young patient's family trusted him—an inexperienced, twenty-four-year-old doctor—with their son's life. They left their son in Dr. King's care and returned to the campground.

A very nervous Steve opened his textbook and prayed and prayed before successfully removing the appendix. The child recovered well, and Steve could now say he had performed surgery on his own. We rejoiced together, and Steve learned to pray with patients and nurses before every surgery from then on, even though every outcome didn't turn out as well.

That same year a local woman, a leader in the community, had come to the hospital with cold symptoms, and ended up dying of a strep infection two days later. Steve was very upset, but he would learn to live with the fact that some patients died, even though he had done his best.

Praying and surrendering situations big and small was intrinsic to our growth as Christians. As a couple, we attended the little Pentecostal church in "downtown" Hazelton, led by Pastor Jack and Erma Williams. They were great friends and a support to us as we found our way as a couple.

That church shines for me because that's where we dedicated our son David to Jesus. He was splendid in a nightgown covered in little Native American scenes, sewn with love by his Grandma Evelyn King. I still have a piece of that fabric in my memory box.

The Highway Leads to Mission City

Soon our season in Hazelton would end. We had been living there for one year when Steve had a major disagreement with the head nurse over some outdated practices at the hospital. We were to learn the hard way that change often comes slowly.

Frustrated, naïve, and immature (we both were—actually 24 and 26), Steve gave Dr. Whiting an ultimatum: "Either she goes or I do." Well, we went, reluctantly so. The head nurse had devoted her life's work to that hospital, so Dr. Whiting could hardly side with Dr. King in his first green year of practicing medicine.

Later Steve often mused that we probably would have stayed in Hazelton for years if it were not for this conflict. Had we been more mature and sensitive to people and the situation (Sorry, Dr. Whiting), the outcome would have been different. However, when Steve said it was his way or the highway, we were the ones sent on the highway.

When we moved from Hazelton, we moved as a family of five: dad, mom, baby David, cat, and dog. But to where?

Steve had explored the possibility of surgical training in England, but that didn't pan out. However, a locum[5] in Mission City, B.C., came to our attention. This seemed like a good solution so we moved to Mission City when David was six weeks old. Steve covered the medical practice for a local doctor, and we stayed in his house.

---

5 Locum: short for *locum tenens*, where a physician fills in for another physician on a temporary basis.

Mission City, now called "Mission", took us due south from Hazelton—nearly touching Alaska—to eighty kilometers southeast of Vancouver. Mission's population of 38,833 was gigantic compared to tiny Hazelton.

Before I tell you about our time in Mission City I want to tell you about two amazing miracles, the birth of my two children: David in Hazelton, and Deborah in Mission City.

Chapter 7

Seventh Heaven—the Miracle of Birth

Bless the Lord O my soul, and all that is within me bless His holy name (Psalm 103:1).

Before David could be dedicated, he had to be born. It was June 19, 1968, when our beloved son was welcomed into this world, a highlight of our lives. Dr. Whiting, the only other permanent physician in the area, took his holidays two weeks early so that he could be present for my delivery. Except his vacation was not quite early enough for my baby boy.

We enjoyed the great outdoors in Hazelton, a beautiful plush green village on the banks of the Kispiox River, framed by snow-covered tree-lined mountains. Often we would relax by hiking the trails.

On one of those hikes when I was about 9 months pregnant, Steve and I were walking in the nearby mountain woods, taking in the gorgeous wildflowers and scenery. As I bent down to pick a bouquet of these delicate floral beauties to bring home for my table, my water broke. "Oops, something is happening," I said. We quickly hurried back to town to collect a few things and then rushed down the path to the hospital.

Dr. Peters, a doctor from India, was interning with Dr. Steve and Dr. Whiting, and she took charge. Through the long night and into the early morning, she kept pressing me to push. "Puuuush, Judy," Dr. Peter urged. "Puuuush ..." It was a long night.

David Stephen King Is Born—Seventh Heaven

In the early morning, Dr. Steve arrived from home just in time for the delivery. Dr. King was patiently guiding Dr. Peters through the delivery process until I was desperately out of patience. "Please, Steve, take over!"

He did and soon enough I heard him forget his doctor role for a minute. "It's a boy!" he exclaimed with glee. David Stephen King had arrived.

We had an issue immediately, since my blood type was Rh-negative and Steve's was Rh-positive. (When the mother is Rh-negative and the father is Rh-positive, the unborn baby can inherit the Rh factor from the father. This makes the baby an Rh-positive too. Problems can arise when the baby's blood has the Rh factor and the mother's blood does not.)

Steve gave David a shot, which was a new antidote just released for these Rh-positive babies. Steve had received the antidote by mail the day before—which he thought would be for another patient. God knew exactly who that antidote would be for.

I was in seventh heaven as they put our little boy on my chest. A miracle of birth! *This is what I was created for*, I thought. I was so happy I can't even explain the feeling. In those days, moms and babies stayed in the hospital for five or six days—what a luxury compared to today!

Phone calls followed by beautiful bouquets of flowers arrived from our family in the East. We took photos of David, had them developed and sent them Eastward. We were far, far from home and family in Ontario, and that was a challenge, but the whole community rallied around us: the church, the hospital, and our First Nations friends.

We loved being new parents and adored our baby boy. I was nursing our new baby and at times so that I could sleep, Steve would get up and do the night feedings, He insisted on doing that since he reasoned that he was on call every other night for the hospital anyway. I think he insisted but maybe that was my desired perception. Wish I could check so many of these details out with him.

Anyway, what a guy and what a father to his baby boy! Steve was a remarkable father from the start. I remember how much he loved cuddling his newborn son.

We only had about six weeks in Hazelton as new parents. On one occasion, I remember taking our baby on his first outing to a local outdoor rodeo at the fairgrounds. As a first time mom with no family around to advise me, I had my baby bundled up with a bonnet and sweater and blanket in the carriage.

As I recall, the temperature was in the mid-70s or 80s. Funnily, one of the more outspoken town ladies all decked out in cowboy boots and hat approached us to admire our baby and said, "What in the world are you trying to do, suffocate this kid?"

I explained that I didn't want the baby to catch cold and she laughed and said, "Would you want to wear a wool hat and sweater and blanket today?"

Our time in Northern B.C. was happy in so many ways. I have all positive memories, except for the time Steve was Santa Claus at the hospital Christmas party, and all the sweet young nurses sat on his lap and kissed him on the cheek. Perhaps that wasn't the best memory, especially since Steve had clearly enjoyed himself immensely. I believe we had words about it—Bah, Humbug! Otherwise, Hazelton was the perfect place for us to grow in our marriage and grow as a family.

Faithful friend, faithful Spike

Our black lab, Spike, was a delight. When David was born, I spotted Spike from my second-floor window of the hospital and waved to him. "Spike!" I called as his tail wagged happily.

The next thing you know, Spike was parked on the fire escape ledge outside of my hospital room window on the second floor—and wouldn't leave until we did, five days later. Well, at least he was there every time I looked out! I'm sure he was up and down.

Whenever Steve would have to go to the hospital at night, Spike would accompany him down the path and wait outside the hospital door until Steve was done.

When I got a job for the government as a social worker supervising the First Nations families in their homes, Spike would join me on my visits and keep my car seat warm while I went to check on my families around the village. For those first six weeks of David's life, Spike would sit guard by the baby carriage during the baby's outside nap times.

Upon leaving Hazelton, and before Mission City we decided to take a road trip back to Toronto to show off our precious three-month-old son, David Stephen King, to the family in Toronto.

Everyone was excited. I remember stopping at a gas station right before we got home to change my baby's clothes into a new, fancy outfit. David looked cute and I was so proud of him.

We had a wonderful time showing off our baby boy to all of the relatives on both sides of the family. Of course, the family was delighted. It was so much fun for me to visit old familiar sites.

I remember specifically a walk to Wanless Park with my Grandfather Turner (my mother's father) who was in his nineties at the time. We strolled together, pushing the stroller, reminiscing and him delighting in this his beautiful baby great grandchild. It was the last time I would see him.

From Hazelton to Mission City

When we returned from Toronto to our new home in Mission City, I found out I was pregnant with my baby girl—"Irish twins" they call two babies so close together. The trip back across the thousands of miles was, of course, tedious and challenging, because I was newly pregnant. But once we had found housing and settled in, we were excited. I enjoyed my pregnancy and was healthy, energetic, and happy.

We were still a family of three (not counting Spike and Sam), with Steve and I adjusting to being parents and all of us adjusting to our new surroundings in the forests and mountains of the Fraser Valley. Again, we found fulfillment in working with and befriending the First Nations people.

At Christmas of that year, we hosted five or six of the Native kids from the nearby residential school that we had gotten to know. We baked cookies together, hung stockings with them and gave them Christmas presents to unwrap. We were very moved to see the joy on their faces on Christmas morning.

Of the teens in Mission City, one stands out in my heart: Pamela, a girl who lived on a rundown farm with her elderly parents, across the street from us. We became friends, she spent time at our house, and we brought her to church with us.

She joined the youth choir that I was leading and came to understand personally, God's love for her. I can still hear Pamela singing the lyrics of one of our choir songs: "Nothing is impossible when you put your hand in God's; nothing is impossible when you trust his Holy Word."

We hadn't yet been missionaries overseas. But I guess we can all be missionaries wherever God has planted us. At times the most important thing we can do for him is simply cross the street.

Seventh Heaven Again—Deborah Kathleen Is Born

By far, the most important sentinel event of our time in Mission City was the birth of our cherished baby girl, Deborah Kathleen, born on May 27, 1969.

Deb, whom I lovingly call "Meem," has always told me that I look at life through rose-colored glasses and forget the pain of the past, which may be partly true. But honestly, I had a good pregnancy and easy labor with her! I loved being pregnant.

My labor began in the early morning, and when we arrived at the hospital, my doctor came to check on me. "You'll be a while, yet," he said. "I have to perform a surgery, and when I'm done, I'll check in on you again."

The nurses called him while he was getting scrubbed up for surgery and told him to come quickly. Deborah was born ten minutes from his first examination, at 9 pounds, 14 ½ ounces. Since Steve worked at the hospital, everyone was very excited. They gave him a pink carnation to wear along with his beaming smile.

I was ecstatic to have my beautiful baby girl. As I looked down at her tender face, I was sure that she smiled a toothless grin back. In those days, as I've said before, you stayed at the hospital for days on end, enjoying meals served to you, warm, soothing sit baths, and your baby being brought from the nursery to mom (babies stayed in the nursery, not their mother's room like today).

I nursed her as I did David for three months, even though the nurses tried to convince me otherwise. It's a curious thing how baby care changes through the years, with different stages of what's good and what's not.

Baby Deborah was a delight and such an easy baby to take care of. As with David, she slept early through the night cuddled into her bassinet right beside our bed.

Grandparent Kings

Grandma and Grandpa King came from Toronto to help us, and I think they stayed about a month. They were a tremendous help to us then and on many other occasions. I am very grateful for their help and their loving contributions to our children's lives. Both David and Deborah have countless fond memories of them.

Our first call whenever we were going to travel and needed baby-sitters was to Mom and Dad King, who were always there for us, and would later even travel to the North West Territories to help. In fact, when David and Deborah were helping me sort through family stuff when I moved in 2014, we came upon a cassette of Grandpa King singing his made-up ditties and Scottish (his birthplace) songs to the kids when they were young. What a treasure!

We would make cassette tapes for our parents with singing and greetings and send them to Toronto and a month later we'd get one back with their news and songs. Three years ago, when Deb discovered this cassette, she made a recording on her iPhone and sent it to her King/White cousin Ellen in Germany, all in about thirty seconds. That's progress, I guess.

Back to my delivery of Deborah. I luxuriated in the hospital with my precious newborn baby girl. When I returned home on a Sunday morning, Gramma and Grampa King and brother David were there to greet us with lots of love and also home cooked Gramma meals. Probably, shepherd's pie, candy apple pudding or even oat cakes and sausage, gramma's specialties.

I happily settled in as a mother of two. Of course I'd had an easy delivery and 7 days of rest and vacation at the hospital, so different from today when new mothers are rushed home with barely a day in the hospital. And I also had the best loving help in the world with Gramma and Grampa King. They were amazing grandparents, and

I and my children will always be grateful to them for all of their love and incredible help and grand parenting.

That year in Mission City with our two babies was wonderful, challenging, satisfying, and life-changing. Over the years I have affirmed the privilege of motherhood to many young moms. It is one of the most important, challenging, and rewarding roles that a woman can have.

Chapter 8

Renewal at Miracle Valley

While he was eating with them, he gave them this command. "Do
not leave Jerusalem, but wait for the gift my Father promised,
which you have heard me speak about. For John baptized with
water, but in a few days *you will be baptized with the Holy Spirit*
(Acts 1:4-5). [Italics mine]

During Steve's month-long locum in Mission City, we learned of
another opportunity to do further work with the indigenous
peoples at a substance abuse facility located nearby.

One of our concerns in working with the 1st Nations People in
Hazelton, was the tragic growing incidence of alcoholism. We both
were interested in becoming more educated in the treatment of this
insidious family-destroying disease.

Steve accepted the offer to become the director of a Salvation
Army rehabilitation center called Miracle Valley, especially after his
disappointment in Hazelton. Miracle Valley was located in a beautiful country setting, with lush surrounding forests, rolling hills and
refreshing streams.

The rehabilitation center housed men with binding addictions
who were taken off the streets of Vancouver. The men were provided
with nutritious food, counseling, spiritual healing, medical treatment,
and work skills. And a great number of them were healed. What an
honor to be a part of that effective ministry!

Spiritual Renewal

God orchestrated that we live in Mission City at this specific time, 1968-1969 fellowshipping among people of his choosing and of course, enjoying our two babies, David and Deborah. He had heard the yearning of our hearts, and He placed handpicked individuals in our lives to teach us more about him.

Growing up in a Pentecostal church, I had been baptized in the Holy Spirit and had spoken in tongues as a teenager. Although I really didn't understand this gift fully, I appreciated in a deeper way the reality of the Holy Spirit, whose purpose is to magnify the Lord Jesus Christ, who magnifies and listens to God the Father.

I had experienced a special awareness of God's presence, and Steve had always been drawn to that in my life. He wanted to know more about the Holy Spirit and his role in our lives. So, in the shadow of God's handcrafted mountains, we searched for his Spirit's hand.

Sven Soderlund, a longtime church friend from my childhood and teenage years, was studying at Regent College in Vancouver. He came to dinner one night and we asked him a lot of questions about the Holy Spirit. He suggested that we read the book, *They Speak with Other Tongues*, by John Sherrill.

Sherrill had been an investigative reporter who examined the gift of tongues and eventually became a Christian through his research. We eagerly bought the book, a bestselling Christian classic now, and in its pages we found answers to many questions.

God continued to orchestrate, writing the "score" of our time in Mission City. We met Captain Lesley, a Salvation Army officer from Vancouver who had been on the verge of leaving the ministry because of discouragement and burnout. When he experienced this "Baptism of the Holy Spirit," he was renewed and refreshed in his faith.

Other officers, including our dear friends Al and Peggy Ryan began having prayer meetings to seek the Holy Spirit. Revival was happening, and we were caught up in its waves.

Our next step on the journey was a short trip to the U.S., just over the B.C. border. We were encouraged to attend Rev. Dennis Bennett's Episcopal Church in Seattle. He wrote the classic book *Nine O'clock in the Morning*. For the first time we heard a congregation singing in tongues, worshipping God in their heavenly language. It sounded as if we were in the Presence of God hearing the angels worship and sing.

These experiences converged in a question: How could the gift of tongues be more important to me? Steve was hungry for more, seeking truth with his whole soul, and I was wondering why it didn't seem to mean as much to me. Why didn't the gift make more of a difference in my life?

"What should I do?" I asked the Lord.

"I've given you a gift and you haven't used it," He replied. "Of course, it hasn't made a difference." By the way, I didn't hear an audible voice, just that nudging of strong thoughts that come with listening to God.

I thought about this in terms of my university research studies. "Okay, God, I will practice this gift for ten minutes, three times a day, for a week. If I see a change, I will commit to praying in tongues for the rest of my life."

That week of practicing my gift was exceptional. Sharon, an older lady for whom I had been praying, approached me seeking answers about God, and I had the opportunity to lead her to Jesus. Pamela, the young lonely teen I had befriended gave us an open door to invite her elderly parents to consider Christianity. But the biggest event of all was what happened to Steve.

There was a Salvation Army prayer meeting and we debated who should go since David was only six-months-old. Deborah hadn't been born yet. We decided that we'd both go and put the baby to sleep in his pack-n-play there. Steve sat in the center of a circle and the Army folk laid hands on him and prayed for him. This new language just poured out of him. He immediately began to speak in tongues.

That night, after the meeting, every time I awoke in bed, Steve was praising God in tongues. It was like a dam had broken. He was being refreshed, renewed, and anointed in ways he had never experienced before. He was so full of love for others and me, it was incredible. (Several years later, Steve wrote a paper entitled "Neurophysiological Considerations of Glossolalia," and he presented it to a Christian medical conference.)

During this extraordinary week of renewal, I learned that there are two types of tongue experiences noted in the Bible. The Apostle Paul said, "I speak in tongues more than you all" (1 Corinthians 14:18). I believe he is referring to a heavenly language given to enlighten us to pray in the spirit when we don't know how to pray and don't have the words, sometimes it's just groanings, and at other times what seems like an unknown language.

The second type of tongues is the spoken gift, in a public service for the edification or benefit for those present. When there is a spoken gift of tongues, an interpretation should always follow (1 Corinthians 14:13). Paul tells us to desire spiritual gifts, but the best is prophecy. When a tongue is given and then an interpretation, it is a prophecy and a Word from the Lord for his people.

I have experienced both gifts. Let me emphasize here that experiencing God's gifts does *not* make one a special person; these are gifts from the Father that are freely given in response to the asking from an open dedicated heart.

One does not have to be in ecstatic, emotional prayer to use the heavenly language given to us. According to Steve's paper and other articles and books, the tongue can in this instance bypass our emotions. It helps to pray in our heavenly language when we don't know how to pray, or when we are down or depressed.

In later years, both Steve and I silently practiced our gift of tongues in our work as mental health professionals. We listened to people's stories while at the same time trying to listen to the Holy Spirit. Over the years, sometimes more, sometimes less, this gift became a part of our spiritual armor (Ephesians 6), i.e., "praying at all times in the Spirit."

We also became involved with the Jesus People during our year in Mission City, worshipping with them around a fire with many musicians strumming their guitars to simple worship songs. Many churches had sadly turned away these scruffy, long haired folks because of how they looked.

Our friend James Thomas was one pastor who opened his doors to these fiery new converts, and many of these nontraditional people became strong Christian leaders as time went on. It was another reminder to us that man looks on the outward appearance, but God looks at the heart.

Another change and another move.

After one year in Mission City, Steve was approached by a leader from the Pentecostal Assemblies of Canada (PAOC), which had just one mission hospital. It was located in Canada's North West Territories, in Hay River, 400 miles north of Edmonton, Alberta. (If you look at a map, it's actually north of the 60th parallel!)

Hay River was at the end of a gravel road—as this gentleman informed us, there were no roads beyond. The hospital desperately needed a medical doctor, so by God's direction and grace, we responded to that call. Another adventure!

Chapter 9

The Road Stops Here—Hay River

The weapons of our warfare are not carnal but are mighty to the tearing down of strongholds (2 Corinthians 10:4).

David was fourteen months old and Deborah was just three months old when we packed everything up for the long, two-day road journey north to Hay River.

This was quite a big move with two babies, but luckily, we had Jennifer, a young woman we had met through the Jesus People. She had been a nanny in England and was looking for her next steps. She offered to travel with us and ended up staying with us in Hay River for a couple of months, expertly helping us until we were settled.

On the way, we stopped in High Level, Alberta, at the Hudson Bay Company store to purchase parkas, snow suits, hats and gloves, long underwear, and anything else we could think of to prepare for the cold weather, which could dip down into -50 degrees Fahrenheit in the winter. When I zipped up my navy parka hood, trimmed in white fake fur, it covered every part of my face except for my eyes. This was helpful in a place where one's nostril hairs would freeze instantly upon stepping outside.

We arrived in Hay River in the month of August. Its population was about 3,000 people, with roughly half the population made up of

Indigenous peoples[6], mostly Métis and Inuit.

Our family moved into a cozy, three-bedroom, colonial type mission home, right across from the doctor's office and next door to the nurses' residence. (For a joke we sent our concerned big city families a photo of a run-down log cabin, captioning it, "Our new home.") We had baby sitters available anytime, as the young nurses—far from home—loved to come to our welcoming home for some nurture and love. I loved the company.

We'd hear complaints from Steve's U of T medical school classmates living and working in Toronto, that they never saw their children. They'd be on call at the downtown Toronto hospitals and would have to stay all weekend.

On the other hand, Steve was home for supper every night and could tuck the kids in at bedtime. He crossed the street every day for lunch, or we would go to him. The little ones and I would bake cookies in the afternoon and take them to serve the patients in the waiting room and give Daddy a treat.

Steve even brought the children to work with him sometimes. David was his "assistant" on a call to sew someone up, and he loved to introduce little blonde, blue-eyed Deborah as his "nurse" on visits to a Native village. The Indians loved that.

Since we had no television, and only one radio station—the CBC—there were few distractions. At night, after we tucked the kids in, Steve would pick up his guitar and we would sing for a while. One night we heard a chirpy little voice from a girl we thought was fast asleep. "Sing 'Thy Loving Kindness,'" she requested from her bed upstairs. I still think of Meem when I hear that song.

You might wonder why I still call Deborah "Meem." That name originated when I had two babies in highchairs hungry for breakfast and eagerly waiting for their turn as I alternated a spoonful of Pablum (a smooth Canadian rice cereal) to each of them. That's when little Deb would say, "Me, Me, Me," and I coined the name "MeMe."

"OK, MeMe, open your mouth like a little birdie; here it comes." Later we shortened it to "Meem." I still call her Meem. She remem-

---

6 The term "Indigenous peoples" is a collective name for the three groups of original peoples of North America: Indians (sometimes referred to as First Nations), Inuit, and Métis.

bers her dad shouting above all the other parents at swim meets in high school just before she dove in: "Go, Meem!"

Despite the polar bear weather, I took the kids out almost every day (partly for my sanity), bundled up in several layers, as we'd go for a walk on the toboggan. In the winter we had to keep our car running at the grocery store or the engine would freeze. There were no worries about someone stealing our car, because there was no place for a car thief to escape, with one slow road coming in and the same slow road going out.

The one grocery store in town was severely limited in its offerings. One year, Steve had an upcoming birthday, and I wanted to cook him Chinese food as a surprise since the only restaurant in town was the local bar, which boasted hamburgers as their main menu item.

I ordered the ingredients far in advance and they arrived by transport plane just before the big day. There were water chestnuts, Chow Mein noodles, and Sesame oil. The cooking took a couple of days, so it was the last time I did that! When we moved from the North it was much more fun to order take-out, certainly no work, and even less expensive.

As good as life was in Hay River, there were times of acute loneliness as well. I dearly missed my family in Toronto, who seemed light years away. Once, the parents of one of the young nurses came from Ontario for a visit, and she sent them over to my house for tea. When they arrived at the door with hugs, I burst into homesick tears. They put their arms around me like pretend parents and we enjoyed our tea party and conversation.

Revival

Spiritually, Hay River was a time of empowerment and miracles. Steve and I led the youth group at our church, and when we would hold all-night prayer meetings, the presence of the Lord was so palpable no one wanted to leave.

One night while we were praying, a young teenager named Sharon gave a message in tongues. We had a young guest that night, Jacque, from Paris, who had been a patient at the hospital and was invited to the meeting. Jacque had been presented with the Gospel at the hospital (most of the staff were missionary nurses or doctors) and he came to the meeting seeking answers to his spiritual questions.

Sharon spoke English only, but her message in tongues was delivered in perfect Parisian French. Her message answered Jacque's questions specifically in his native tongue and accent. He fell on his knees in surrender to the Lord. That was an amazing demonstration of one of the gifts of the Spirit according to its scriptural mandate.

Approximately 60 years later, in 2017, when I attended a reunion of Hay River folks, I met Sharon, now a senior lady and grandmother herself. "Did that really happen?" I asked her.

"Oh, yes" she replied. "I remember the incident clearly and have told many people about it."

Spiritual Warfare

As a teenager I had experienced God's power in answer to prayers mainly modeled by my mother. I will always be grateful for the example that she was to me with her faith. As I mentioned before, my mother had taught me to pray about everything.

However, I had never even considered the whole subject of spiritual warfare. I didn't know what it was, I'd had no teaching on it, and the idea of the demonic was an enigma to me. The following dramatic experience landed me on a very steep learning curve.

Every year a revival meeting was organized for the town's people and a Native evangelist from the south was invited to speak. The children and I had joined the group as campers, on the Hay River island campground consisting of rustic log cabins. We were there during the day and Steve would join us at night.

A young woman named Cynthia had come as a visitor from Regina, Saskatchewan, a city in the south of Canada. Long ago she gave me permission to tell her amazing story. When I greeted her, introduced myself, and put my hand on her shoulder, I must have said something like, "Isn't it great to know Jesus"?

When I spoke the name of Jesus as I touched her shoulder, she immediately fell on the ground and writhed like a snake. In a nanosecond, I sensed the Presence of Jesus standing on my right beside me and out of my mouth came the words, "In the name of Jesus, be free."

Without further ado, she got up, shook her head and I was able to lead her to faith in Jesus. Jesus delivered her immediately. The compassion that I felt coming from Jesus to this dear woman was beyond description. It was just like the story in the Bible when Jesus heals the person who was possessed with a demon, the demoniac. And it had *nothing* to do with me. I was clueless, but Jesus had the power and the compassion to go with it.

The Native evangelist had witnessed this event. "Sista King," he said in awe, "I believe you have a ministry of deliverance." *Thanks a lot*, I thought, *whatever that means*! I didn't know what to do with that proclamation. I was just a 26-year-old mom with a couple of toddlers running around and I had *never* experienced anything like this. I don't think that at the time I even knew what spiritual warfare was.

This was my first—but not my last—experience with overcoming the powers of darkness with the stronger power of the name of Jesus. It sparked my interest in later years when both Steve and I became very involved with Dr. Neil Anderson's Freedom in Christ Ministries. More on that later.

> Submit yourselves then to God, Resist the devil, and he will flee from you. Come near to God and he will come near to you (James 4:7).

After experiencing these new supernatural and demonic experiences, we had lots of questions. We noticed in a Christian magazine that there was going to be a conference in Miami, Florida, with some of the speakers like Derek Prince, Charles Simpson, and others known for their books on spiritual warfare.

We were hoping for some answers and instruction in this whole area of spiritual warfare. So we flew to Toronto from Hay River, left David and Deborah with their two sets of grandparents, and traveled to Florida for this conference of several thousand people.

Interestingly, the theme of the whole conference was on love, not spiritual warfare. Little did we know that this whole conference was for us! We needed to exhibit the fruits of the spirit, as we became more aware of the gifts of the Spirit.

We had been impatient with our fellow church members when they questioned and criticized us for being so excited about our deepening faith and belief in the gifts of the Spirit. We needed to experience more balance. God freely gives us his supernatural gifts. Practicing these gifts of the Spirit in ministry should produce more fruits of the Spirit. Sadly, we often get this out of balance, and we had done just that.

P.S. – I know that I was often a failure in this regard, finding it much easier to practice the gifts of the Spirit in ministry outside of the home, than in practicing these gifts in the home amidst the nitty-gritty of marriage and parenting.

Christian Medical Foundation

Another God incident happened and, in retrospect, maybe that was another reason that we had attended that conference in Miami.

We started talking to some folks who were sitting close to us in the conference hall. One of the women was Kay Reed. She told us about her husband Dr. William Standish Reed, a surgeon and author, well known in Christian circles as a doctor who prayed for his patients and had seen many miracles of healing.

Kay invited us to come to Tampa and stay with them at the Christian Medical Foundation where healing prayer services in the beauty of the Anglican Church tradition occurred regularly. So we changed our flight home from Miami to Tampa, rented a car, and had an amazing time of inspiration and encouragement with Bill and Kay Reed.

They became lifelong mentoring friends to us. In fact, at one point we were planning to move to Florida to work with the Reeds in ministry and medicine. Steve even studied and wrote his Florida medical board exams to get a Florida license and we applied for immigration to the USA. We never got to Florida, but that's a later story.

God plants seeds of growth, change, and guidance in various ways and through various people. God certainly used Bill and Kay Reed. After that first visit to Tampa we regularly attended yearly conferences with doctors from around the world that believed in prayer. Bill's (Dr. Wm. Standish Reed) book is called *Surgery for the Soul.*

Over the years we learned volumes from Bill and Kay about God's ability to heal the sick. Bill liked to say, when praying for someone to be healed: "We have not because we ask not. I'd rather err on the side of asking rather than not asking. Then it's up to God what happens.

I've been obedient. I can't heal anyone; only God does that."

This is a lifelong lesson I have gone back to countless times. Bill saw many examples of supernatural healing and encouraged us along the way to explore it as an option. His example planted a seed in Steve's heart.

My husband always wanted to know more and experience more in the healing ministry of medicine and in supernatural healing. He had a hunger and thirst for more of God and together, throughout our marriage, we dug into these topics together. What an amazing blessing that was for me, and what a great time we had together visiting healing ministries around the world.

Music in Hay River: The Hay River Centennial Choir

The golden thread of music continued to flow during my time in Hay River, a village north of the 60th Parallel on Great Slave Lake. I taught music in the schools, led the church choir, played piano, and performed the occasional solos.

The mountaintop moment was related to my work with the Hay River Centennial Choir. The choir was comprised of about a hundred voices, plus or minus, which seemed to me like everyone in town. We sang original folksy songs about the development of the Northland. Here's a snippet:

> "North of 60 lies a land that is wide and free and grand, and we call it ours no matter where we roam."

Here is an excerpt from the jacket of the LP record of the choir performing:

> The Hay River Centennial Choir was organized in the spring of 1969 to honor the past and herald the future of this last Canadian frontier. The choir, comprised of children from three Hay River Schools, is augmented by the voices of adult Territory residents. Members of the 96-voice choir sing of their love of the north in fifteen original compositions. "North of Sixty" the Northwest Territories' official Centennial song, beautifully records the mood and color of this rugged land. Lyrics and music depict the fierce patriotism of the northerner—his love of the great white expanses and of the bigger land of Canada.

A year after the choir was formed, our friend Reverend Bob Jackson, who led the choir, moved out of Hay River. I was asked to lead, an opportunity which I gladly accepted. Since most of the nurses from the hospital were also singing in the choir, the head nurse scheduled her nurses into our home for baby-sitting to fit their hospital schedules.

The members, including Steve, wore a uniform of dark slacks, locally-crafted beaded caribou leather mukluks, and white fox-fur-trimmed parkas. We would go on to tour across Western Canada, performing concerts in Winnipeg, Saskatoon, and Calgary. We even recorded a Long Playing Record. I still have a copy of this record which contains all of the songs of the Hay River Centennial Choir.

Presented to Queen Elizabeth II

Nothing touched the day the queen came up north, June 11, 1970, and the Hay River Centennial Choir gave a command performance in Yellowknife, the capital of the North West Territories. (I just noticed that date—June 11—is the day of our wedding anniversary. How cool a gift is that?)

The government of Canada had invited us. I've been known to tongue–in-cheek gleefully brag about this "command performance." The truth is: in all of the NWT the competition was *zero*.

It was exciting. We were in a flurry of preparations and practicing when we heard Queen Elizabeth, Prince Philip, Prince Charles, and Princess Anne would be coming to the Arctic to celebrate the previous bicentennial.

The choir traveled in specially chartered jet planes across Great Slave Lake to the capital of NWT—Yellowknife. As the conductor of the choir, I was presented to the Royal Party by Jean Chretien, who was at that time Canada's Minister of Northern Affairs and later became Prime Minister of Canada.

After we performed our forty-five-minute concert, the presentation took place. Left to my own nervous devices, I might have happily hugged the royals, but thankfully the government gave me a few lessons in protocol, including how and when to curtsy. It took all my restraint not to dance up to them!

The Queen, the Prince of Wales, and Prince Charles and Princess Anne politely and coolly complimented me on our performance, but

Prince Phillip was very outgoing and chummy. He was so enthusiastic and warm in his comments and questions about the choir that I offered to bring our choir to the castle for a concert. I can't remember his response after my "blurt" but I surmise that he smiled and that was it. He never did take me up on my offer, though wouldn't it have been amazing if he had?

After that pinnacle experience, the choir wanted to stay together and learn new music, so we continued for a few more years. That year (1970) I wrote a Christmas Cantata which the choir sang, and it was broadcast on the CBC on Christmas Day. That was a great opportunity to spread the good news of Jesus in a predominantly secular country. Also at the time, "Up with People" was popular so we continued to practice and perform some of that music.

A postscript:

In 1995, Steve and I flew to our old home in Hay River and attended the 50th anniversary of the hospital. I gathered some of the old choir members and we reunited for one more performance. What joy for me to lead this choir again after so many years! I was so pumped!

***

Most folks would never choose to live north of the 60th parallel in the frigid temperatures far from most civilization. Yet it was a magical place that stirred and challenged us and brought out our inner ruggedness.

Miles from anywhere—literally—we and our neighbors forged an incredible sense of community. We celebrated our holidays together, we worshipped together, and we prayed for each other. We simply dressed for the cold and found we could live, work, and play in it quite easily.

One payoff was the spectacular light show we could witness most nights. In the central Northwest Territories, the Northern Lights are visible for an average of 200 nights per year. That's nearly every single night of the late summer, autumn, winter and early spring! The Aurora felt like another miracle in a place filled with them.

Hay River was perfectly placed for maximum viewing enjoyment. There we had clear skies, ultra-low humidity, and a location beneath the band of peak Aurora activity—the so-called "Auroral Oval." The most common color was an eerie, wild, green, but sometimes, during Aurora storms, the sky would blaze bright crimson and purple. It was truly amazing and moved our hearts to praise the Creator. Yes, it was cold, but oh, what a sensational view we had, just by looking up at the sky.

Musing

I'm so grateful that God, the Holy Spirit, desires to bless us with his gifts to glorify Jesus and to edify the body of Christ.

Chapter 10

Flying High in Hay River

These signs shall follow those who believe (Mark 16: 17).

Gazing upward to God's Northern Lights was glorious, but sometimes we got to look down from the sky, as we piloted our small four-seater Cessna 172. Steve and I and the children would fly in our plane to remote Native villages where Steve would provide a medical care clinic.

At first, when Steve told me he wanted to get his pilot's license, I was adamantly against it. It worried me! I was a young mom with two young toddlers and far away from family. What would we do if Steve were to perish in a fiery plane crash? But with lots of prayer and "strong talking" on both of our parts, my mind began to change.

I knew that I had to put my fears aside and go along with my husband's crazy idea. Steve got his pilot's license and I decided I did not want to be left out of the fun. So, I'd pack supplies and my babies, and we'd go with him, flying high over the Canadian arctic and visiting the village peoples.

We forged some good friendships with the nuns, brothers and priests, breaking bread together at their tables. Sister Gagnon of the French-speaking Grey Nuns was the Mother Superior of Fort Resolution. She and I became good friends, exchanging books, hers in French and mine in English.

Once we went on a two-week camping trip by plane down the Mackenzie River. It was just Steve and me. Our two little ones were safe with Grandma and Grandpa King back in Hay River.

We stopped at all the isolated mission settlements along the river, landing on the existing few grass strip runways. We would land and wander into that particular village, with backpacks and Steve's guitar strapped on our backs. God, what adventures do you have for us here? It was always exciting, and I loved every bit of it.

Most of the villages had both a Catholic presence and a Protestant presence, with their separate missions usually located at opposite ends of the village and little or no communication between the "opposing" missions. This emotional wall built between them was because of mis-understandings and fear. This was in the early 1970s when it was very unusual for Protestants to worship with Catholics.

Steve and I would usually visit the Catholics first, with gifts from the Fort Resolution Catholics in the south, and then we would cross the village and visit the Pentecostals. The Protestant missions in the north were Pentecostal. In the evening, we would invite the Catholics over to the Pentecostals and we would host a singsong. Steve would strum his guitar and I'd lead us all in praise songs.

Slowly, reconciliation, understanding, and fellowship ensued, proving that we were one body in Jesus Christ. This same pattern occurred all the way down the river wherever we stopped. It became a pattern throughout our life, to network and reconcile peoples together whenever possible.

Another village we visited was Fort Good Hope, NWT. The priest there was a phenomenal artist, and he had fashioned the church and surrounding buildings from hand-hewn logs. Inside the church hung his masterpieces, including his cornerstone work, a painting of Mary and Joseph depicted as a First Nations couple arriving by canoe to the village to deliver their baby boy.

In this painting, the priest had painted everyone's homes in the background. What a beautiful, culturally relevant portrayal of the nativity scene! We were amazed and blessed to gaze at this master-piece, far from any prestigious museums or galleries and literally in the middle of nowhere.

There were several dramatic moments on this camping trip, but none so gripping as our harrowing near-death experience of flying to Inuvik. It was to be the culmination of our two weeks camping in the arctic, and what a culmination! Inuvik is approximately 100 km (60 mi) from the Arctic Ocean and approximately 200 km (120 mi) north of the Arctic Circle. It's so far north that this area experiences an average of fifty-six days of continuous sunlight every summer.

As we flew up the majestic Mackenzie River, we marveled at the stunning scenery below. But it had been raining, and the rain grew steadily worse as we approached the Inuvik airport. Via radio, we were informed that we were being denied permission to land because of the dangerous conditions, dense fog and driving rain.

I peered outside the window of our four-seater plane and cringed. Visibility was basically zero. To add to our troubles, we did not have enough fuel to turn around and go back. How would we survive? Because we were so close to the North Pole and its magnetic pull, our north and south perceptions were skewed. From one moment to the next, we couldn't discern if we were up or down.

The irony was that we had come prepared, or so we thought. We had tucked a pup tent and some dried food in the plane in case we needed to make an emergency landing. But, as we looked down, there was only muskeg, an arctic type of bog, and absolutely no place to land.

Steve and I both thought we were about to die. We were scared.

As the seconds ticked by, we begged God to spare our lives. We pleaded with the radio tower in Inuvik to let us land despite the warnings, since this was our only option. There was nothing below but muskeg, rocky ice, and irregular terrain. *Jesus, save us! Help us land this plane!*

With only our maps indicating our altitude, and a desperate prayer, we broke through a dark blanket of fog and landed at the Inuvik airport. Whew! When the plane came to a stop, we both exhaled as if we'd been holding our breath for an hour. As we got off the plane on the tarmac, the airport crew raced to us. Both of us were close to collapsing, with our knees like jelly and our hearts madly racing.

We ended up spending the night in Inuvik's lone hotel, appreciating our lives anew, and praising God for our rescue. No more small planes like ours were allowed in or out of that airport for five days, due to the incessant rains. The town was completely socked in, but we were blessedly safe. God is so good.

The next day we travelled over to Tuktoyuktuk, the complementary Eskimo village along the Arctic Ocean coast. This time we flew on a large transport plane. We were told that a local priest at our destination had fixed up an abandoned ship for us to crash for the night with our sleeping bags. We just wanted to explore the village a bit. I also wanted to dip my toes in the Arctic Ocean.

We knew no one there in this obscure Eskimo village. To our surprise and delight, we were met by a young white woman, Janelle, who was married to an Eskimo man. She had heard via the grapevine that a white couple was arriving. Janelle, eager for fellowship, invited us to stay in the home she shared with her husband, Alvin, a shy, handsome man. I have a photo snapped by their newly constructed bungalow: a dog sled and team, and a snowmobile, the old and the new side by side.

Whaling season was about to start so Alvin took us for a whale hunt on his boat. It was a little too early in the season, so we didn't see any whales. But Alvin wanted to confide something to us.

"I am planning a surprise trip for Janelle to see her parents in Seattle," he said a little bit shyly. "But I am afraid. I have never left Tuktoyuktuk and I have a major fear that I will … melt." Bless his heart! We assured him that he was in no danger of melting and affirmed his surprise for his wife.

Steve and I thoroughly enjoyed hearing about Alvin and Janelle's long winter hunts and how they constructed igloos along the trails as shelter. Our time in Tuktoyuktuk with Alvin and Janelle felt like a soft place to land, quite literally, after our near-death experience in Inuvik!

I look back with such fondness now to those experiences, even the scary ones. Oh, what I would have missed if I had dug in my heels and insisted Steve not learn to fly! That decision would have been based totally in fear, and I am grateful God gave me the courage to overcome those fears and trust him. (I did end up taking ground pilot training and practicing some landings, just in case something happened to the pilot!)

We would have missed the masterpieces painted by a humble priest in a Northern outpost. The miracle of being spared from a plane crash. The gentle hospitality of an Eskimo man and his wife in a village called Tuktoyuktuk. And Steve would have missed one of his all-time favorite memories.

Doctor's House Call on a Dog Tea

Steve was flying home from the village one day when a call came over the radio: there was a medical emergency in one of the other villages. Could the doctor come? Since it was wintertime, Steve had to hire a pilot to drop him off and pick him up after the clinic because he couldn't leave his plane parked at the airport. The gas tank would have frozen solid.

In winter the planes were equipped with skis, not wheels. When Steve agreed to make this emergency call, toting his doctor's black bag, the pilot landed the plane in a field on skis. Steve was then met by a dogsled team to transport him to the village.

For the rest of his life, Steve King loved to recount the story of making a house call by dogsled! The patient, if you are wondering, was not in a life or death situation, but was treated ably for her high fever anyway. And Steve had a good story to tell for many years afterward.

***

Miracle of Healing

Out of all the phenomenal things that happened in Hay River, the incident of Steve sewing a man's arm back on ranks at the top. It started out as a simple Tuesday. Steve was at work when a group of men burst into his office lugging their badly bleeding friend.

The man, a native from a nearby village, had been horrifically injured in a mining accident. His entire arm was severed from his body. Steve sized up the situation with alarm. Here was an extreme emergency: a man's mobility and maybe his life hung in the balance.

Steve had only the vaguest idea of how to reattach the bloody arm which the man's friends had brought along in a cooler, in hopes the doctor could work a miracle. He had never experienced anything remotely like this before. He prayed, and called me to pray.

Steve quickly consulted with his intern, an even younger doctor named Sushil Sethi, *aka* "Shelly." They both conferred with their anatomy textbook, looking up all the connecting points in an arm. They would have to match the intricacies of socket and arm perfectly if this man was to have any use of his arm again.

How could they possibly attach all the muscles, nerves, and blood vessels perfectly? With many deep breaths and prayers for wisdom and courage, Steve and Shelly performed the surgery, sewing the arm back on to the best of their ability.

After Steve died, Shelly, now a vascular surgeon, wrote this in Steve's memory book: "Dr. King sent someone to the hardware store to purchase a $1.00 drill with varying sized bits and some dental wire and proceeded to attach that arm."

Shelly also wrote a P.S. to that extraordinary Tuesday: Dr. Shelly was in the Edmonton airport about ten years later and heard someone call out to him. "Hey, Doc!" Shelley turned to see a man standing there, waving enthusiastically. "Remember me? You sewed my arm back on, and it works great. I'm actually working as a mechanic now!" Truly a *miracle* of God.

I wish Steve could have heard this story, but then again, maybe he did, in Heaven. We'll not know for sure until we get there. It was another testimony of God's supernatural power working in the lives of his children.

Only our sovereign, healing God could have used his servants' hands to attach and heal this man's arm. There was simply no human explanation for this. Even if Steve and Shelly had been veteran surgeons rather than green, young physicians, they would not have been able to replace a man's arm that perfectly. Only God.

***

There were miracles galore in the Canadian arctic, but the element that set Hay River apart for us was even more miraculous: revival.

Only recently, while attending a prayer meeting locally, praying for revival in Grand Rapids, did I realize what we had experienced in Canada all those years ago. It was an "Aha!" moment. A friend, a leader in Grand Rapids recently showed a PowerPoint history of Grand Awakenings, historic revivals around the world. My eyes became riveted to the screen. "Revival in Canada: 1971" popped out at me as if in neon lights.

That's it, I thought. *That's when Steve and I were in Canada and had firsthand experiences of so many coming to salvation, of so many signs and wonders, healings, deliverances, and reconciliations spoken of in the Scriptures!*

My heart was filled with thanksgiving and praise to God, who had led us there and allowed us to see his power at work! At once my mind quickened with memories and the many lessons God had for us in Hay River.

Lesson #1: The Power of Forgiveness

Sara was a new Christian in Hay River whom we knew through Steve's work. At one point, Sara had been given an immunization shot by a public health nurse in our village. However, the nurse had given Sara the wrong shot and she experienced a terrible allergic reaction and went into anaphylactic shock.

This was not a one-time thing, as in the aftermath Sara would end up in the hospital every few months. It had been an honest mistake on the nurse's part, but it caused Sara many serious bouts of suffering. Steve was on call one night at about 2:30 a.m. when he was awakened by Sara's husband on the phone. "Sara is having another serious attack and is having trouble breathing."

Steve quickly dressed, and I know that he must have been praying. He headed to her home on the next street, and after giving her antidote for the reaction, he boldly confronted her. "Sara, have you forgiven that nurse for giving you that shot?"

"No!" she said, belligerently. "It was her fault. Why should I forgive her?"

"Until you do," he said, "you're not going to get better." God had given Steve this knowledge and discernment for Sara's situation. Sara was resistant. But when Steve explained that forgiveness didn't mean that she was saying that the nurse was right—in fact, that the nurse had made a serious mistake—Sara reluctantly prayed a prayer of forgiveness and forgave the nurse. Sara never had another reaction again.

In 2 Corinthians 2:9, Paul says, "I forgive so that Satan might not outwit me, for I am not unaware of his schemes."

If we are living in unforgiveness, we give the enemy an opening to influence and damage our well-being, whether it is a physical issue, or a matter of the soul (the will, mind, or emotions). I've seen many people radically set free from physical ailments when they chose to forgive someone and/or themselves. Have you ever heard the saying "Forgiveness sets the prisoner free and that prisoner is me?" So very true.

Lesson # 2: The Power of Jesus as Deliverer.

On another occasion, Steve was mystified by the case of a young man who was not getting better, despite there being no medical reason for his debilitating symptoms. All the tests had been done, so Steve prayed for the man, taking spiritual authority over any evil spirits the enemy may have sent his way, including the spirit of unforgiveness. The young man immediately coughed and sputtered and threw up. The demons were gone and he was healed completely.

C.S. Lewis says that there are two opposing viewpoints that allow the devil free reign. One extreme is blaming everything on the devil or spotting a devil under every bush and not taking personal responsibility for anything. The devil made me do it.

The other extreme is disbelieving the devil exists at all and allowing him free rein to work in the world undetected and unchallenged. Believing in Satan and demons is just hocus-pocus. It's just silliness. Both are wrong and dangerous if we believe in a Biblical worldview. We need to find the balance.

Steve and I began to learn to find this balance in those early days of revival in Hay River. Jesus, as always, was our ultimate role model as he led a perfectly balanced life. A Scripture that spoke to us during this time was Luke 10:17-20. When Jesus' followers came back from a ministry trip and reported how excited they were to see people set free from demons, Jesus exhorted them to be more excited about their salvation than about casting out demons.

The seventy-two returned with joy and said, "Lord even the demons submit to us in your name." He replied, "I saw Satan fall like lightning from heaven, I have given you authority to trample on snakes and scorpions, and to overcome all the power of the enemy; nothing will harm you. However, do not rejoice that the spirits submit to you, but rejoice that your names are written in heaven."

We had to remember that even though we had experienced incredible, powerful spiritual interventions—even the casting out of demons—that salvation in Jesus was our ultimate focus and our number one desire for others.

Lesson #3: The Power of Salvation

Steve and I had friends, Ray and Peggy, with whom we shared some meals and family outings. Peggy was a believer, but Ray, a high school teacher in our village, was not.

One evening service at the church Peggy got up and shared a tearful prayer request to the congregation: "My husband is lost and needs to find Jesus," she cried. "But it seems so hopeless. And our marriage is unraveling."

Peggy's plea for prayer was so earnest, so heartfelt, I will never forget it. We doubled down on praying for Ray's salvation, trusting that God would answer the prayers of his people and of his child, Peggy.

When New Year's Eve came along, we invited Ray and Peggy over for a celebration. Ray, who liked to cook, baked me a chocolate birthday cake for my birthday the next day—such a lovely surprise. As the evening went on, I don't remember any of the specific conversation, but I have a vivid image of Ray kneeling at our tattered brown chesterfield (sofa) on his knees, asking Jesus into his heart. What joy!

***

Marian was a teenager who had come to live with us for the summer. We were fond of her and prayed often for her salvation. At this same time, we had been involved with a situation involving one of our Christian nurses at the hospital, her husband and the Jehovah's Witnesses religious cult.

In our view, the JWs had stolen one of our sheep, the nurse's husband, and we wanted him back in the fold. We knew the leaders of the Jehovah's Witnesses in our area through our community involvement. One evening, we invited these leaders over to our home for a Bible study.

In their minds, they would be the ones converting us. Nonetheless we felt we should open the Scriptures to them and let God handle the rest. During the study, we could hear Marian creeping quietly up and down the stairs through the living room, where we were having our meeting. It was obvious that she was listening to our conversation.

Throughout out discussion, we had been continually coming back to this verse in John:

> "I am the resurrection and the life, he who believes in me though he is dead, yet shall he live and whoever believes in me shall never die" (John 11:25).

"Do you believe that?" We would ask the JW leaders. Sadly, to our knowledge they never did embrace the truth of the gospel.

When, after tea and cookies, our friends left to go home, Marian came downstairs. "I'd like to become a Christian," she said. "Will you pray with me?"

It was marvelously simple: The Word of God empowered by the Holy Spirit had done the work, and Marian was ready to receive salvation in Jesus Christ. Later, we had the joy of baptizing her in the chilly waters of Great Slave Lake.

***

We met Victoria, a Catholic sister, when she ended up in the hospital with a suspected suicide attempt (although when she and I were reunited in the fall of 2017, thirty-seven years later, Victoria told me she had not attempted suicide, but had been very depressed).

When Vickie was released from the hospital, we invited her and the local Catholic priest to come to our home for a Bible study. Victoria ended up coming to deep faith in Jesus that evening. She left the convent, got married some time later, and she and her husband served the people of China as missionaries.

***

Lesson # 4: The Power of Healing Prayer Coupled with Medical Intervention

It was during the end of our time in Hay River that we learned another valuable lesson. Steve had injured himself while lifting a heavy patient in the hospital and had developed a painful inguinal hernia. We'd seen so many examples of supernatural healing during that time that he was passionately sold on the idea of God healing him.

"Maybe I should just be a praying, healing evangelist instead of a doctor," he mused. God was leading in that moment, but not the way we expected. We called the elders of the church to anoint Steve with oil, and after anointing him, and many prayers of healing and confession, Steve still had the hernia.

"Why don't you just have the surgery," Steve's doctor friend, Dr. Sethi, questioned him. "It's a simple surgery and I can do it for you."

Steve had the surgery, which was a success. My husband was healed in a different way. We again realized the blessing and healing of medicine and surgery. God was showing Steve clearly that he had called him to be a doctor, a healer to many through medicine accompanied by prayer.

Steve and I had experienced so many amazing things during our time in Hay River: God saving us from plummeting to a fiery death from a plane crash; Steve and Shelly impossibly reattaching a man's arm; Sara's healing; God's supernatural intervention with the man who threw up the demons; leading Marian, Ray, and Vickie to salvation in Jesus. To us, all these powerful events fell under the umbrella of revival.

One definition of revival is this: "a reawakening of religious fervor." We had been a part of a great awakening, and it had been glorious, wondrous, and astonishing. As the years progressed, and we reflected on those amazing, high-flying Hay River days, we wanted to experience the same kind of spiritual potency again. Steve and I longed for those days, and quite frankly wondered if we were doing something "wrong" in our present lives in Grand Rapids because we weren't seeing those "signs and wonders" as before.

Oh Lord, search our hearts for any impediment to your power! We prayed. But even though we did—and I do—encounter God's wonderworking power at work in our lives, nothing has ever touched those four and a half years in an arctic outpost. There has been nothing quite like the revival that swept across Canada, and swept across us, ever since.

Musing

Lesson learned: The power of forgiveness, the power of deliverance, the power of salvation, and the power of healing (supernatural and medical). Oh, Father, Lord Jesus, and Holy Spirit, what an amazing God you are. Hallelujah!

Chapter 11

Intensive Spiritual Training

And I will do whatever you ask in my name, so that the Father may be glorified in the Son (John 14:13).

God works in mysterious ways, and He had something very different for us next: A new time zone, a different nation, and poles apart weather! We loved Hay River dearly, but God seemed to be leading us somewhere else.

While living in Hay River, we heard about Christ for the Nations Bible Institute (CFNI) in Dallas, Texas, a Bible college that proudly promoted the Bible as their main textbook. Something ignited in our hearts. They offered a one-year Bible intensive, so we jumped at the opportunity.

"I've spent so many years studying medicine but little time studying the Bible," Steve said.

So, with a wind and a sail, our "yellow box," (a car carrier which Steve made from old coffin crates delivered to the hospital) on top of our station wagon, we drove 3,000 miles due south, from Hay River, NWT, to Dallas, Texas, for a year of Bible training.

The box contained all we thought we would need for one year. David was four and Deborah was three. We didn't know where we would be living but we knew it was right for us and somehow we were excited.

Having given away most of our belongings in Hay River, we were free, students again, settling in with our precious kids for a year of adventures. During our year there, truth from our study of the Scripture laid a foundation in our hearts that would last us for the rest of our lives. That year at Christ for the Nations was incredible, inspiring, and fun.

In the spring at CFNI, we were invited to participate in a Jesus March in downtown Dallas. Hundreds of people joined in with placards and signs proclaiming: "God loves you." "Come to Jesus." "John 3:16." "One Way." I can still see my small children, marching proudly, pointing their index finger to the sky, with huge smiles, proclaiming that Jesus is the Way.

Surrounded by believers from all over the world, we lived and studied in an environment that was culturally diverse and had many "mature" students and families, like us.

Before we left Hay River, we had wondered if we might be greeted by a one-room apartment with a hot plate. However, we were thrilled to be accommodated in a two-bedroom apartment—paradise! We loved our little apartment. Steve converted our master bedroom closet into his office and we slept well, except for the one night near the end of our stay when we were awakened by sirens and smoke billowing through our apartment door.

I guess we were all sleeping very soundly because we didn't hear or smell a thing. It took the firemen banging on our door to get our attention. "You must evacuate now!" they yelled. The apartment above us was on fire. Thankfully, all was well, everyone was rescued, and the fire was contained.

Our time in Dallas also invigorated us with a much better understanding of the miraculous and supernatural work of God. Dr. Gordon Lindsay, along with William Branham and Oral Roberts, had originally been active in the "Healing Ministry," having started in the early days the magazine the "*Voice of Healing.*"

It was Gordon and Freda Lindsay who had the vision of starting this interdenominational Bible School that would focus on the Holy Scriptures as the main textbook. Gordon was a prolific writer himself and wrote more than 200 books. Ours was only the 2nd class to have completed the yearlong program.

This class of two hundred students met in a converted nightclub. Now decades later there are thousands of students, and a large modern campus. We certainly were in a laboratory of learning about healing.

One afternoon, Gordon Lindsay, the president of the bible college, noticed Steve was absent from class and swung by our apartment on his way home (he and his wife, Freda, lived in the same complex). Gordon did not know Steve was suffering a migraine headache, a painful ailment he had suffered somewhat regularly for many years.

Gordon marched into our apartment, and with no preamble or talk, laid both hands on Steve. "In the name of Jesus—be healed!" In thirty seconds, Steve's throbbing pain dissolved. We were flabbergasted. He never experienced another migraine headache again except for one short one when we were on a mission trip in New Mexico.

As a couple we enjoyed attending classes together, learning and discussing together the deep truths of the Bible. We were blessed that David could attend a pre-kindergarten class and Deborah a pre-school class during the mornings when we were in class. In the afternoons, besides studying we had fun exploring the sites of Dallas and often swimming in the pools on campus.

We were growing as a family and in our marriage, except for the following laughable experience: but I guess that was a learning experience for me too.

How to be a Good Wife

From the sublime to the ridiculous is this story which I remember with chagrin and humor. It's always good to laugh at yourself.

Having a love of books, I picked up a new 1970s bestseller called "*The Total Woman*," by Marabel Morgan, in which she laid out a blueprint for Christian women to "fascinate" their husbands. Steve didn't notice all the lovely things that I was doing to fascinate him.

But he did notice that I was quite annoyed because he *didn't* notice. Being fascinating was harder than I thought. I was so tense trying to be this ultra-alluring, perfect wife, and yet Steve seemed oblivious.

"What are you trying to do?!" Steve finally exclaimed. When I explained that I was trying to be fascinating, he said, "Just please be who you are—that's why I married you."

Later, we were able to have a huge laugh over the whole stupid thing. Lesson learned: Don't try to be somebody you're not. There are so many voices that one can listen to. Dear Marabel Morgan was not the voice for me.

Listening to God & My Father's Healing

We were learning and being encouraged to listen to God. John chapter 10 became one of my favorite chapters in the Bible. Jesus is referred to as our Shepherd and we, his sheep. "My sheep hear my voice," He said. It's such a tender picture.

I have several little sheep of various sizes on my bookshelves in my office to remind me. Listening prayer and asking our Father how we should pray was beginning to take root in my soul and spirit.

In the middle of our school year, we were issued a mega challenge to ask for God's wisdom and listen for his guidance. A disturbing phone call from my family in Toronto informed us that my father was gravely ill, in renal and liver failure. He was comatose and not expected to live.

My dad had many health problems over the years, including morbid obesity and diabetes, complications from which he had his leg amputated. Steve contacted my dad's doctor, whom Steve had known from his internships in a Toronto hospital, and asked about my dad's condition. Should we come home?

"Yes, come as soon as you can if you want to see him alive," said Dr. Volpe. "He's in the ICU and I believe he's dying." All four of us jumped on the next available plane and flew home to Toronto.

Once on the plane, Steve kindly suggested he sit with the kids so I could sit alone and pray and process what was happening to my father. As I sat and prayed and asked the Lord how to pray, two Scriptures came to my mind:

You have not because you ask not. (James 4:2)

And I will do whatever you ask in my name, so that the Father may be glorified in the Son. (John 14:13)

I asked the Lord, "Well, what is your will here regarding this situation?" And He brought another verse to mind instantly:

This is good and pleasing in the sight of God our Savior, who desires all men to be saved and to come to the knowledge of the truth. (I Timothy 2:3-4)

I knew my father did not have a personal relationship with Jesus. He hadn't kept us from church, but most often he would stay home and cook a roast beef dinner for us, probably one of his love languages. Dad loved his food—we all did, and I still do.

I believed my father was going to accept Jesus as his Savior because of the verses God gave me. I also knew, according to those Scriptures, that it was God's will that Dad be healed, even for a few minutes so that he could make that important choice and decision.

I know now that this was a gift of faith from the Holy Spirit because I could not have mustered it up on my own. I was very scared. With promises of the Word resonating in my heart, I arrived at the hospital to see my mother standing outside my father's room. She rushed up to me. "Judy, what is going to happen?"

"Mom, he's going to be healed," I said with a quiet confidence.

My mother relaxed, but the rest of my family, some of whom were not believers at the time, tensed up. "Don't give her false hope!" they exclaimed, annoyed. "We just got her used to the idea that Dad was dying!"

Things got uncomfortable quickly as some of my siblings, annoyed with what they thought was my false hope, said, "Who do you think you are, marching in on your white horse, proclaiming Dad is going to be healed?"

I was shocked and devastated because I loved my brothers and sisters. I was close to each of them, certainly in different kinds of ways. I wasn't trying to come in on any kind of white horse, proclaiming healing; I was just trying to be obedient to what God had put in my heart.

For three days, Steve and I sat by my comatose father's bed in the ICU, praying and reading Scriptures aloud and singing to him. My dad always loved my singing. When I was a university student in Toronto, he would sometimes drive me down to the campus. On the way, in the car, he would say, "Sing to me, Judy," and I would.

The Sunday we were in Toronto, Agnes Sanford, an early pioneer in the healing movement, was speaking downtown at a large Anglican cathedral. My mother, sisters, and Steve and I attended this service in hopes of obtaining some healing for my father.

Sanford was the wife of an Anglican priest and had written many books on healing, including "*The Healing Light*." At the service, she announced that we could come up to the front of the church and stand in proxy for someone who needed healing. In her teaching, Sanford exhorted us to ask God how to pray and for God to give us a picture for that prayer.

Since I am a visual learner, I have found now that God often speaks to me in pictures and visions. As I was being prayed over, standing in proxy for my father, I asked for a picture from God. The picture I received was of a man in the ICU sitting up in bed reading a newspaper.

We left the church and went directly to the hospital to visit my father. We pushed open the door expecting to see him lying in bed in a coma, but my dad was sitting up, eating a fried chicken dinner with green string beans.

You would think my first thought would be a shocked and ecstatic "*Oh, wow! Dad's out of his coma!*" But oddly enough, my first thought was "*Why would they give a man coming out of a coma fried chicken and green beans, not Jell-O and consommé?*"

Lord, forgive me. You healed my father amazingly! My dad lived for eight more years as a believer in Jesus Christ. He was spiritually healed and saved, and he was also physically healed.

Later, he told me something astonishing: "When I was in the coma, I saw myself going down a funnel to hell, and I could see Jesus at the top of the wide end of the funnel, summoning me. I was descending into hell and darkness and, as I looked up, I could see the figure of Jesus getting smaller and smaller. At one point I looked up and said, 'Yes' to Jesus. Yes—to Jesus, and salvation, and eternity!

"At the moment I said 'Yes,' I felt a large hand grab me and swish me up by my shirttails and all of a sudden I was conscious."

He awoke in his hospital bed, spared from death and hell and given a new chance at life. Thank you, Father. My father's life was changed in that instant. His remaining eight years on this earth were quite a different experience from his first lifetime, without Jesus. He and my mother had some sweet, mellow years after a long difficult marriage. It was a gift for everyone who loved them, including me.

Mexico

Back in Dallas, we had settled in with an amazing group of friends, including Gordon and Freda Lindsay, who became our dear mentors. Everyone called Freda "Mom Lindsay," because she nurtured us all. Gordon prayed for hours a day and had written, as I've mentioned before, over two hundred books. They were known around the world as people of great faith and prayer—early movers in the charismatic healing movement.

Freda got the idea that at Christmas vacation Steve and I should drive her and Gordon to Mexico, to see our missionary friends, the Wayne Meyers family and then go on to Acapulco. She wanted Gordon to be around our four-year-old son and three-year-old daughter, to get used to children because they were about to become grandparents. We had a great trip, stopping along the way in the Mexican villages.

Since we didn't have reservations in Acapulco, we were taking a chance, and indeed the first night there was a disaster. We learned something, though, in our stay in that second rate, dusty, moldy room with paper-thin walls: make reservations! No one slept very well. However, through the thin walls we could hear dear Gordon Lindsay praying and interceding all through the night. I wonder how Freda managed to sleep through these nights of prayer with Gordon.

The next day, Freda had a proclamation: "God, who owns the cattle on a thousand hills" could provide us with a lovely place in which to stay. And that He did. I remember having Christmas dinner on a beautiful patio overlooking the Pacific, with waves rippling and dolphins dancing. Every soft breeze whispered to me: See, God does provide!

Israel

In March of that year, we were invited to join the Lindsays in leading their annual Israel Tour. This was a huge dilemma for me. Who would I entrust to take care of the children? I didn't think I could leave them with strangers. Our favorite baby-sitters were Steve's parents, and I would have been much more comfortable leaving David and Deborah with them. But Steve had invited them to come on the trip with us as a gift to them!

It was heart wrenching for me to leave my babies behind and go so far away. We arranged for a trustworthy young couple, Wayne and Jill, to stay with them, but the night before leaving I was weeping on my knees, not sure I could leave them.

I made the kids a cloth calendar, like an advent calendar, with little pockets and a wrapped gift for them to mark each day we would be gone. The pockets held a special pencil, lifesavers, a package of gum, a little car, a barrette, balloons, a ball, a skipping rope, crayons, a coloring book, etc. It comforted me to make it and think of my little ones receiving their surprise each day.

When we left them, the kids were both crying and so was I. It was *so* hard. But God did a kind thing for me. On the Dallas Freeway, on the way to the airport, we passed Wayne and Jill's car on their way to Sunday school, going in the opposite direction. We could clearly see the kids in the back seat laughing at something! It was so sweet, and God's way of saying, "Mom, the kids are going to be fine. Trust me."

They had *seemed* fine, but I learned 47 years later that it apparently caused some emotional baggage that my adult children were still carrying with them. I guess the above description is part of my looking at life through rose colored glasses, believing what I wanted to believe.

That's also known as denial. When my grown children read the above description, they described how our leaving was a very traumatic experience for them of abandonment, fear, and constant tears. David, not quite a year older than Deborah, recalled how he had to continually comfort his sister.

I feel so badly about that decision. In retrospect, I wish that I had *not* left on that trip. My children were too young—3 ½ and 4 ½—and I would certainly not recommend leaving children that young for almost three weeks. I should have followed my heart instincts. That's a hug regret, *not* a miracle!

The Bomb

Unfortunately, we were in for a surprise once our flight was underway. We had just arrived at La Guardia from Dallas. We were on the tarmac, heading overseas on Alitalia Airlines, seat belts buckled, ready to take off, when sirens began to scream at top volume.

"Evacuate the plane immediately!" was blared over the loudspeaker. There was panic everywhere. Once out of the plane we were briskly escorted into a roped-off lounge and told that there had been a bomb smuggled onto the plane.

I looked around. There were frightened mothers with small children, older seniors with terror on their faces, and tense police scurrying around. I started to sing and lead people in songs they might know. "Kum Bay Ah," "Amazing Grace," Christmas carols, "O Sole Mio" (after all, this was an Italian plane). I sang every song that popped into my head.

The crowd calmed down and for two hours, while the bomb squad searched our aircraft, I kept the people singing. So my theory is: If all else fails, sing. "Thank you," the airport personnel encouraged me several times. "Please keep it up. It's helping." I should have asked for a free ticket!

Finally, they told us that they had found and removed the bomb and that we were all safe to board the aircraft. We boarded the plane—with significant hesitation—and flew safely to Israel via Italy. Thank you, Lord.

Israel was amazing, especially in the middle of studying the Bible at CFNI. Sister Lindsay had me leading singing on the bus or anywhere else for every occasion.

"O Little of Bethlehem" as we approached Bethlehem. "I Walked Today Where Jesus Walked" as we traversed the stony road of the Via Dolorosa—the way of suffering. "Fill My Cup, Lord" while at the location where Jesus' encounter with the woman at the well took place.

We sang in the Spirit as we worshipped and prayed in the Upper Room. We sipped the most delicious, strong little cups of espresso, which were offered to us at the merchants' stands. The hospitality and the people were delightful. There was the baptism in the Jordon River, the exquisite experience of Masada, and then swimming in the Dead Sea.

Wow! I have one hundred slides to prove how incredible this trip was. The Bible came alive for us in a new and dazzling way. And the kids (at least physically)—and mom—survived our separation.

Looking back, it was such a blessing to join the Lindsays on the last trip Gordon would ever take. Two weeks later, during praise and worship at a school service, Gordon slumped over in his chair on the platform and died immediately.

Steve ran to the platform from the audience and administered CPR while the other ministers were praying over him. But Gordon was already in Heaven.

"I knew when I saw him that he was dead," Steve told me later, "but with all of those faith-inspired healers praying over Gordon, I didn't want to be the hindrance of him being raised from the dead."

Steve rode with Freda in the ambulance and was able to minister to her. That event caused us to become even closer to Freda. Steve had become one of Freda's heroes. My husband offered to come to her apartment across the quadrangle and pray for her each nighttime, so she could sleep. We ended up serving our dear friend in this way for many weeks.

Years later, when we would visit CFNI and be in the audience, Freda would always recognize Dr. Steve King in the same way she would recognize the likes of Pat Robertson or Benny Hinn, famous speakers and authors. Freda became one of my beloved spiritual mentors until her death in 2009 at age ninety-five.

After Steve died, Freda wanted me to move to Dallas and be on staff at Christ for the Nations. I didn't make that choice, but I was invited numerous times to travel to Dallas and speak to the student body, the pastoral school, healing conferences, and women's conferences. Up until her death, Freda was a driving force of faith, creativity, and prayer, a beacon to all she encountered. What an example for me.

I was invited recently to speak at the 2020 Voice of Healing Conference in Dallas. So our connection goes on. I don't know if I would ever have had any of these adventures on my own. I'm thankful for Steve and his adventurous spirit which I caught and enjoyed.

In summary, three examples of healing:

1. Instantaneous for Steve's migraine
2. Progressive for my dad's physical healing and salvation
3. Instantaneous trip to heaven for Gordon Lindsay

A small world vignette: By the time I was invited by Freda to teach, I was very involved with the Freedom in Christ (FIC) Ministry. I would teach Freedom in Christ to the students along with sessions on emotions, anger, depression, and healing. Later, I gave a friend, a pastor from Grand Rapids, my FIC training material, so he could teach it in Uganda. When Bob was in Uganda, one of the Ugandan pastors responded immediately.

"Oh, I remember this!" he said. "When I was in Bible school at Christ for the Nations, a lady came and taught us the "Steps to Freedom." What a small world. That was such an encouragement to me. My teaching actually took!

***

Upon graduating from CFNI, we moved back to Hay River for the summer and stayed in the Reimer's home, since as teachers, they had gone south. There was always a need for another doctor in the North. Incidentally, that was the summer that Marian became a Christian after listening in on our conversation with the Jehovah's Witnesses.

Chapter 12

Miracles & Lessons

Thus Judith called on the God of Israel (Judith 10:1 – The Jerusalem Bible).

At the end of our summer appointment in Hay River, we travelled back to Toronto. We left David and Deborah with the family while we flew to Tampa, FL, to attend the Christian Medical Conference.

Before we left Toronto, I overheard a chat between my dad and his granddaughter, Deborah. My father loved the way her eyes sparkled when she smiled and adored interacting with her. "Sweetheart, where will you be moving next?" Papa Briggs asked her.

"I don't know," Deb didn't miss a beat. "Wherever God tells my daddy to go."

Saskatoon, Saskatchewan

She was right. We were trying to follow God's guidance, not knowing what was next for us. At the conference in Tampa, we met Dr. John and Faith Merriman, who offered Steve a one-year residency in cardiology at the University of Saskatoon, Saskatchewan, and we figured that this seemed to be the next step.

Since we didn't have any furniture, God provided an opportunity for us to housesit a lovely, spacious home close to the Merrimans. The fully furnished house belonged to a professor who was on a one-year sabbatical. Yeah, God!

During that year on the Canadian prairies, we had another life-changing healing experience which comes alive to me again as I write. Our friends, Al and Peggy, from Miracle Valley, B.C., asked us to pray for Al's sister, a young, forty-something mother of four children who lived locally and was having heart surgery.

"Would you please visit her before the surgery and pray for her since we can't be there?"

Of course Steve and I were glad to do this, and we visited this lovely woman, inviting her Catholic priest to come and pray with us. It was encouraging for us to hear Al's sister, Marjorie, affirm her personal faith in the Lord Jesus. The surgery had a reported 50/50 mortality rate. As we were fresh from a faith-believing Bible school, we were sure that the odds for healing would be much better.

Steve and I did everything we knew to do. We fasted. I got a baby-sitter, so I could intercede at home by myself. We mobilized prayers from every Christian we could think of. Steve asked if he could scrub into the surgery because he was a friend. Everything was in place for a positive divine healing result. During the surgery, Steve called me with concern.

"Keep praying—they can't stop the bleeding." In the operating room, he asked if he could openly pray over her bleeding heart for healing, and with courage and boldness, Steve prayed in the Spirit over her, begging for her healing.

However, sadly, Marjorie died on the table and they could not resuscitate her.

"Why, God?" the two of us were devastated. "We thought we did everything we were supposed to do!" Disappointment and doubt filled our hearts. Not wanting to give up, I boldly proclaimed that, at the funeral, Al's sister would get out of the coffin and walk down the aisle, a modern-day Lazarus. This would be the miracle of healing that God would do!

I went to the funeral with great expectation, but that lovely young woman did not get out of the coffin. Denial again?

Major Lifelong Teaching

God had something to teach us from this experience. That same day in the afternoon we attended the wedding of a young First Nations couple, new friends of ours in Saskatoon. The best man got up during the service and sang as he strummed his guitar.

"I have decided to follow Jesus … no turning back, no turning back."

As he sang, God spoke to my heart: "Have you decided to follow me because I do miracles and healings, or have you decided to follow me because I am God?" Those words are etched in my spirit. I knew in that moment how presumptuous I had been. I was chastised, but it was discipline wrapped in all the love in the world, a *rhema*, a living word from God.

I don't know why Marjorie was not healed, even though she had a 50 % chance of a survival, but I was comforted by the fact that she was with Jesus in her heavenly home.

There is a lesson for me in here. We cannot put God in a box. We can't presume, as I did, that if we do all the right things we would always get what we want. Then, may I ask myself, *Who's in control?*

On the whole we enjoyed the year in Saskatoon. David started kindergarten, and I liked our church, participating in the music program and ladies Bible study, and performing with the Saskatoon Symphony Orchestra.

One memory stands out from all the rest: I went to pick David up from school, and when he saw my car he started running across the street. At the same time, I saw a bus coming towards him and my blood froze. Then, before I could act, I saw a big hand stop that bus within inches of David.

I wonder how many times throughout our lives God has protected us from danger and even death? I believe this happens much more than we believe. By now, dear reader, you probably have your own stories of witnessing God's mighty, miraculous hand. What has God done for you?

Banff, Alberta—1972-1976

When we still lived in Saskatoon, we heard about an opening for a doctor in Banff, one of the most famously beautiful places in the world.

Adding to the appeal, Steve and I had a growing vision of starting a healing center that was holistic, ministering to the body, the soul, and the spirit in a beautiful, creative, and life-giving atmosphere and setting. We wondered, was this spot in the Rocky Mountains the perfect place? We prayed about it and decided this was a great opportunity to explore our vision for a healing center.

So we checked out Banff and decided to move there. It was difficult to find housing, being in the National Park. We were finally able to rent a two bedroom apartment. Our abode was a section of a log duplex on Muskrat Avenue not far from the town Center.

Steve began his work in private practice with a local doctor and the town hospital. In this popular skiing resort/community, he became very adept at setting and casting broken bones—which were plentiful.

If there had been the Internet in 1974, and we had googled "Banff," we would have come across this alluring description:

"Banff National Park consists of 6,641 square kilometers of unparalleled mountain scenery nestled in the heart of the magnificent Canadian Rockies … Snow-capped peaks, glistening glaciers, and sweeping vistas are just one part of the allure of Banff National Park."

Sounds enticing, doesn't it? And it was.

Banff inspired us all in different ways. As a family, we reveled in the playground that was our backyard, finding many opportunities to get outside and enjoy nature. From hiking in the mountains (where little Deb would collect frogs and save them under her hat), to jumping (not for long) in glacial waters after a hot, sweaty hike. We'd often cook dinner outdoors on our Coleman stove just to be outdoors somewhere in the woods. We made the most of living in such a surreal setting.

Other memories shimmer, such as Deborah walking the block to her kindergarten class at a church just down the street and talking to me on her snack "banana phone." Or David winning the Halloween costume contest with his clown get-up and telling the press he wanted to be a "mischaenery (missionary) clown" when he grew up.

Once, when I had stayed up all night working on my first painting, David told his teacher that his mom had "become an artist last night." I took art lessons in the morning and then painted at home in the afternoon with Deborah. Perhaps this was the beginning of

Deborah's own artistic career, which has beautifully carried on to her own daughters.

We loved worshipping at the Banff Presbyterian Church, where Steve and I taught Sunday School and taught the children multiple Bible verses which we turned into songs or you might say, "ditties." At one point, those lovely rambunctious kids could sing over a half-hour's worth of Scripture set to music.

Professionally, our two years in Banff were a mixed bag. Steve, who set many broken bones from ski accidents, also worked in a general practice and found it wasn't the best fit for him or for the other doctor.

On the other hand, I enjoyed a part-time job working for the renowned Banff School of Fine Arts, coordinating the music for the Canadian Festival of Youth Orchestras. (I continued this position for ten years, even after we moved to the U.S.)

The four of us were happy, but it's hard to plant roots in glorious Banff. Because the town lies in a national park, it's impossible to buy a house, so we would end up renting two houses. As a resort town, Banff is also a very expensive place to live, with sky-high rent and even inflated prices on everyday items such as a gallon of milk (Today, for example, a gallon of milk in Banff costs over $9 CDN).

It became clear to us after a while that Banff would not be the permanent place for us, but it was great for a stopover. After moving there, we realized that our vision of opening a healing center would never work in a place where we couldn't buy real estate. Besides, our dreams were changing as we considered what was next for our family.

We began to think about relocating to Florida, to work with Dr. Bill and Kay Reed and the Christian Medical Foundation. We had attended their medical conferences in Tampa, and Bill and Kay had become good friends and mentors. It was hugely appealing to work with physicians who believed in God's healing power.

We desired a work environment for Steve that integrated good medicine for the body, good psychological treatment for the soul, and spiritual intervention for the spirit. Maybe this would be the environment for that healing center that we had envisioned!

We leaned heavily towards Florida and our desire to work with the Christian Medical Foundation. Steve had already passed his Florida Medical Board exams in order to move to Tampa. We had applied for immigration papers but had been waiting overly long to be approved to work in the United States.

On paper, we had all our ducks in a row. Steve had proof of a job in the United States, and the support of a senator friend of the Reeds who was lobbying the government on our behalf. Yet we were not given permission to immigrate and move the Florida. Our wait ended up being over two years.

Psychiatry or Not?

As we waited, Steve was leaning toward obtaining some training in psychiatry, since he had encountered many patients with psychological problems in his private practice. He began to explore psychiatry as an option.

When our dream of moving and working in Banff seemed to be falling apart, things were falling into place! Matthew 6:33 says it all: "Seek ye first the kingdom of God and all these things shall be added unto you."

"You want to go into psychiatry?" I was concerned. "I don't think that's a good idea."

It was the second time Steve had brought up his budding desire to explore the possibility of becoming certified as a psychiatrist. It was a sensitive topic for me, because I thought at the time that all psychiatrists were nuts. I was a little fearful of another change and the unknown.

Steve was calm as usual in his reply. "This posting advertises a psychiatry residency with a 'religious orientation,'" he said, yet determined. To a point, I understood his desire. He wanted to be equipped to help all of his patients. The posting was for a mental health facility in Grand Rapids, Michigan, 2,000-plus miles from our current home in postcard-perfect Banff, Alberta.

Grand Rapids, Michigan

In February of 1976, Steve decided to fly to Toronto for a medical course and take a short road trip to Grand Rapids to check out the psychiatric residency program through Michigan State University at Pine Rest Christian Hospital.

At this point, Steve and I were on the same page, and I was open to his pursuing some psychological training. We would also be closer to our extended family in Toronto, just a day's driving distance away, and to both of us this was a huge draw.

Steve took his aging parents with him on the seven-hour drive from Toronto to Grand Rapids. He was impressed with both the city and the program at Pine Rest, and when he returned home to Banff he enthusiastically suggested Grand Rapids might be our next home. At peace with this decision, we decided to make the move, believing that, if this was God's will, we would get our immigration papers in time.

It certainly was a test of our faith. Steve resigned from the Banff medical practice in April, and he moved to High Level, Alberta, to work as a *locum tenem*, filling a medical need there. The locum provided his housing and paid extremely well. God was providing for us in our next assignment from him. (We learned "assignment" terminology from our Salvation Army friends, who talked about getting their "marching orders" from God.)

High Level, of course, was the location where we had made a pit stop years earlier to stock up on winter provisions for life in Hay River. Our children were in first and second grade, so I stayed in Banff with them. We did, however, travel to this muddy frontier town for spring break and I was not a happy camper that week.

It was cold, dreary, colorless, muddy, and depressing, and I complained to my family in a way that was quite memorable, apparently. When one of the founding townspeople asked David what his mother thought of the town, he was clear: "She thinks it's a dump!" he said, much to this staunch woman's disapproval. Perhaps not my best moment of winning friends and influencing people!

We made plans to move, and the time to leave Banff got closer and closer. Yet we did not have the proper immigration papers to be able to leave. We chose to believe in the God of the impossible, who had given me the verse "He is able to do exceedingly abundantly above all that you could ask or think." Based on this verse, which I repeated over and over until it saturated my spirit, I had peace for the move.

So I was planning to move to Grand Rapids. Much to Steve's annoyance, I even invited any number of friends and family to come for a visit to our future home—a home we had yet to find, in a country we had yet to gain legal entry! In my mind's eye, I could even see some of the amenities of the house.

"Come visit!" I told people. "We'll have a guest room (which we'd never had in Banff) and a fireplace (one of my desires for a long time)."

Exactly one week before we were to leave for Michigan, our immigration papers appeared in the mail. God is never late—He proves that over and over. His hand kept us from moving to Florida, where, incidentally, the Christian Medical Foundation later ceased to exist because of lack of funds and support.

Musing

I know that God heals, but in the experience with Marjorie, I learned that He wanted me to trust him because He was God and not because of what He could do for me. This was a much deeper lessen that I needed to learn—to trust him in the mystery of not knowing.

Chapter 13

More Than We Could Imagine

To him who is able to do immeasurably more than all we ask or
imagine, according to his power that is at work within, to him be
glory in the church and in Christ Jesus throughout all generations,
for ever and ever. Amen (Ephesians 3:20).

On June 7, 1976, we crossed the border in Montana from Canada
to the United States.

After five long days of playing school, listening to cassettes, nap-
ping, playing "I Spy," reading the Narnia tales, and everything else we
could devise to entertain children(a seven and an eight-year-old) on a
long road trip, we arrived in Grand Rapids at about 8 p.m.

It was raining. A driving, pelting deluge, and we could hardly
see the road through the frustrated and tired windshield wipers. We
peered through the rain at our new home city and saw only dreariness.
Exhausted and deflated, we yearned for a place to rest for the night.

Mind you, this was long before the days when you could look up
a Trip Advisor-ranked hotel and book it with one tap of your mobile
phone. I had to hop out of the car at every motel and walk inside to
check it out and see if they had any vacancies.

On our marathon road trips, it was always my job to find our
nightly accommodations, probably because I was the fussier one. My
one travel tool was a motel guide which I would consult as we drove,
searching out places that seemed decent enough, had a color TV (we
didn't have one at home), and landed in the right price range.

That night my motel guide failed me; I didn't even have a short list of motels to try. We knew no people for hundreds of miles. And it weighed on us all that we had no place to stay, not just that night but any night. The kids were done in the back seat. We were all done.

All my excitement lost air like a deflating balloon. I was depressed, confused, and anxious, trying to hold back tears as I diverted my gaze out the side window, so that the family wouldn't notice. At least so I thought.

Oh, Lord … what have we gotten ourselves into? Jesus, help me! Those three words again.

We pulled off the highway to west 28th Street and drove slowly, squinting through unrelenting rain and hoping to find room at the inn—any inn! Upon spotting the Gateway Motel, we pulled in and hoped for a good outcome. I puddled through the rain to the office and noticed that there was a Bible on the counter. Wow.

The lady behind the counter happened to be the owner. "Are you a Christian?" That was my first question, not "Do you have any vacancies?"

"Yes," she said, nodding, and smiling a curious smile. Something inside me relaxed a bit. Here was a sign of God's care and leading. In Canada, you never saw a Bible on a counter in any motel or hotel. I think I burst into tears and threw my arms around this dear lady in my relief. I'm sure she was shocked.

Mrs. McCaskill became my first friend in this foreign country as she handed me a key to our room with a kitchenette. The motel was right beside McDonalds and right across the street from Long John Silvers. Both magnificent eateries now within walking distance and our diminishing budget!

Mrs. McCaskill even had a singing Schnauzer dog named Pepita, who fascinated David and Deborah with her ability to sing. "Sing, Pepita!" At that command, darling little Pepita would lift her snout in the air and, yes, sing.

The day after we arrived at the motel, we noticed that there was a swimming pool, but alas, it was not in service throughout our stay. Another alas: our station wagon would not start! It was rebelling and also very tired from the trip. It was hot and humid in the high 80s, and the only place to rent a car at that time was at the airport.

We didn't know a soul, except for the motel owner, and so had no way to get to the airport. The Kings were stuck. Uber was still a few decades away, though why we didn't call for a taxi I don't know. I settled us in to the motel as best I could, and we savored the local cuisine of fish 'n' chips and hamburgers.

Steve and I had been reading a book by Merlyn Caruthers called "*Praise the Lord Anyway: How to Turn Your Irritations into Spiritual Motivations.*" If ever there was a time where a book title matched our exact situation, this was it.

We had plenty of irritations, but the book said, by praising God in the mess, we could convert our bad moods to divine inspirations. Easier said than done. So that day, we decided that whatever happened we would choose a positive attitude and praise God. *Oh, brother!*

The sunshine beaming brightly in the blue sky the next morning after a sleep, in contrast to the dull, depressing weather of the night before, had helped, I guess. I wish as I look back that I had remembered this spiritual principle more often.

The spiritual principle is: if we praised God and thanked him for who He was, despite our feelings, God would honor our praise with his help. We sat on the grass surrounding the motel's pool and decided to have an outdoor Sunday school lesson by singing some of our Scripture songs. We were trying to be upbeat but it was difficult.

Our first answer to prayer was that Mrs. McCaskill offered to lend us her car. Can you imagine loaning your car to strangers? But that's exactly what this openhearted dear woman did. There was no such thing as *Zillow*, so we hopped in our loaner and roamed around the town, hoping to spot signs in yards advertising open houses.

The first open house we found was in Kentwood, not far from the motel. Inside the house, we noticed a hymnbook on the piano. "Are you Christians?" The homeowners not only said they were believers, but after hearing our story, they invited us to their church the next day and for Sunday dinner. God was caring for us through the kindness of strangers, and it warmed our hearts and encouraged us.

We ended up staying in the motel for two weeks, venturing forth every day to look for a house to buy. We arrived in Grand Rapids on

June 18, 1976. On the following Monday we met with the Westdale realtor in his office. The secretary had a very sing-song-y voice, which she used to answer the phone and trill the words, "Good morning, Westdale" a gazillion times.

As the week wore on, with no success whatsoever, we forgot to praise God and caved in to discouragement. We had to find housing in a hurry. Steve was slated to start his residency by July 1, and the moving van with our belongings was scheduled to arrive in Grand Rapids on June 28, a date that loomed in our near future.

As Steve pointedly reminded me, I had told the moving company that when they arrived in Grand Rapids we would have an address. "You and your big ideas," Steve declared. I was angry and discouraged. What would Merlyn Caruthers say about us now? Our irritations were turning into unspiritual responses.

With mounting tension and pressure to be settled, we decided to rent an apartment. "*What about the big house with the guest room and the fireplace that I promised all our friends?*" I wondered. Ugh.

We were grumpier by the hour, but God was working amid our foul moods and lack of faith. He even sent a traveling evangelist and his family to stay next door to us in the motel. In the mornings, as we faced another grueling day of house hunting, they would hear us on the path to the parking lot and pop their heads out their motel room door: "We're praying for you!" they cheered. In our relationship my tendency was to be optimistic and Steve's tendency was to be pessimistic, but even I badly needed cheering.

On the next week following Monday, we were on our way to deliver a check to secure a deposit on an apartment when I made a quiet ambivalent suggestion: "Let's just take one more drive over to where the Christian school is, to see if there are any houses close by for sale?" I said.

I was intrigued by the idea of a Christian school. I didn't know there was such a thing and thought it would be great for the kids, and even better if they could walk to school. By that point, this seemed like a long shot, but I've always been one to ask big. Everyone groaned.

It was already dusk, and the kids were weary of looking at houses. I was clutching to very thin threads of faith and recognizing this niggling feeling that maybe renting an apartment wasn't the "real deal" for us.

Steve obliged me, and we took a detour to cruise the area by Sylvan Christian School. We stopped at the corner of Griggs and Philadelphia, one block kitty corner to the school. There stood a 1941 house on the corner, with turrets and handsome lead pane windows. In the front yard was a For Sale sign. I nearly jumped out of the car.

"Please, let's just stop and look at it," I said. The house looked unoccupied, so we decided to poke around. The kids elected to stay in the car rather than view yet another house. They probably felt as hopeless as we did.

When we walked around the house, we saw to our delight that it had a swimming pool, even though that amenity had seen better days. Pieces of random lawn furniture with algae and other green, slimy things growing through them bobbed on top of the murky water filling the pool halfway. I could see the possibilities.

We guessed that there were several bedrooms according to the windows, and a chimney poking out of the roof indicated that the house had a fireplace too. Steve and I looked at each other in the darkening nightfall. "I think this is our house," I said, with growing excitement.

"We'll give a call to the realtor when we get back to the motel." Steve said. That was before cell phones of course.

Together, we walked back to the car and I told the kids that we had found our house. We called the apartment and cancelled with them, and then called our realtor and asked him questions about the house. "That house hadn't come up in my search because it was below the budget that you gave me," he said. Even better! We had never owned our own home before, so it all seemed quite momentous.

After a rather sleepless night, we toured the inside of the house the next day and made an official offer, which was accepted on the same day, a Tuesday. We had the exact amount of money, earned during Steve's locum, for a down payment.

That Friday, our moving van arrived at 1531 Griggs, and the movers were able to unload our belongings from Banff into our new abode. The owners were Christians, and not only allowed us to move in early before the closing, but also offered us pieces of furniture left over from their parents' recent move. In fact, the now refurbished and retooled buffet and china cabinet are still in David and Julie's house to this day, over four decades later.

When I surveyed our new home, with its five bedrooms, three fireplaces and a pool (which wasn't even on my wish list but was supplied), I thought again, *He is able to do exceedingly abundantly above what you could ask or think.* Though my faith had flagged badly, the dream God had planted in my heart of a hearth and home in Grand Rapids, had come true just in time. *Thank you, Lord. You are always faithful, even in spite of us.*

Three days later, when Steve started his residency program, he had a home to return to at the end of the day. Dr. Bill Van Eerden was to pick Steve up for his first day, and I was quite relieved to see that he looked like a normal guy, not the weirdo shrink I had feared. Bill would become an essential person in our lives as a supervisor for Steve in his residency, and later for me as an MSW student when I interned at Pine Rest and eventually became a member of the staff.

Bill was on the cutting edge of learning and integrating the Christian worldview with good psychotherapeutic methods. We had lively and inspiring discussions and I felt affirmed and encouraged by this doctor who knew me and my work so well. In fact, Bill was the one who introduced us to Dr. Neil Anderson's books about spiritual warfare and freedom in Christ.

Both Bill and his wife, Connie—who also became our dear friend—have graduated to their heavenly home. Along with Steve and so many other loved ones, they have seen the face of Jesus, incomparable for them but sad for us who are left behind. Yes, it's a delight for them but a loss for us. After Steve died, Bill continued to be my psychiatric supervisor as I stayed on in my mental health practice.

Yes, little did we know on that first dreary evening what Grand Rapids and its citizens would come to mean to our family. On Griggs Street, our first order of business was restoring the pool back to its former glory—not an easy task. But the result was well worth the effort.

Countless birthday parties, hospital parties, and family parties were celebrated in that pool as we splashed and played and grilled hamburgers and lazed in the sun. Numerous visitors arrived from

Canada and other places to enjoy our guest room. And myriad times I basked in front of one of three fireplaces.

For eight years, we found our haven on the corner of Griggs and Philadelphia. God came through at the last possible minute, testing our faith and showing us again that He can always do more than we can think or imagine.

Musing

I'm so glad that we have a God who never gives up on us, even in spite of our faltering faith. He is there for us. Never give up hope. Jesus promises that He will take us by our right hand and that at his right hand are pleasures for evermore (see Psalm 16).

Chapter 14

Growing in Grand Rapids

His divine power has given us everything we need for life and
godliness through our knowledge of him who called us by his own
glory and goodness (2 Peter 1:3).

In our first ten years of marriage, we had moved ten times: from
Toronto to Victoria; from Victoria to Hazelton; from Hazelton to
Mission City, B.C.; from Mission City to Hay River, NWT; from
Hay River to Dallas, TX; from Dallas to Hay River; from Hay River
to Toronto; from Toronto to Saskatoon, SK; from Saskatoon to Banff,
AB.

And finally now from Banff to Grand Rapids, Michigan! Lots of
adventures but also lots of changes.

As I look back, it probably took its toll, but overall it was fun and
definitely not boring. I probably experienced some stress but believing
it was God's will, coupled with my tendency towards denial/optimism,
I soldiered on. Praying together about these moves really helped me.
I found very early on in our marriage that when I was stressed or
unhappy, I could go to Jesus, who said he would never leave me. That
had been burned into my spirit, as I've said earlier, as a young child.

In each place God had something to teach us and to demonstrate
his power and loving presence. I'm thankful for that. As a young girl,
I couldn't ever picture myself living in one place forever, enclosed by
a white picket fence. So these moves were exciting, and I always tried
to be on the same page with Steve, as he experienced restlessness and

uncertainty about his place in the field of medicine, which made him want to change jobs so often.

And so we settled into the house God had given us at the very last minute. Over the eight years on Griggs Street, we reflected many times on the way we found our home—or more accurately, the way God led us to our home.

David and Deborah started school at Sylvan Christian School, entering 2nd and 3rd grades respectively, and I was hired by the Grand Rapids Symphony as Assistant Manager to Ned Crouch. It was a fulltime job, which we needed because Steve was basically a student himself and only drew a small stipend. We also needed the money to pay for Christian school tuition.

I worried about being gone when the kids would come home from school, but again God provided. Enter "Aunt Kary," an older lady who lived right next door; she became available to come over to greet and watch the kids after school. She provided a quality of care that blessed us all, sometimes baking cookies with David and Deborah and—my favorite—sometimes even making us all dinner.

My job required many evening concerts, so often I would drag the children to work with me—and drag, they would probably agree, is the right word. They would go backstage at intermission and visit with the Concert Hall's stage manager, Abe, a lovely man who often produced "extra" tickets for the Ice Capades or the circus, a happy perk for the kids.

I stayed in that job for a full year. It turned out to be more than full time; it was probably about sixty hours per week. I had to be at every "home" concert and even the run-out concerts, wherein I would accompany the musicians on the bus and manage their concerts in other cities.

The second year I took the job as education coordinator because that was more part-time. My work involved scheduling the symphony quartets, brass and wind ensembles into schools, and creating a Saturday morning mini-symphony concert opportunity for preschool and elementary school children.

Our first concert series was called "Piccolo Pete." In that concert the symphony played "Jack and Jill at Bunker Hill," by Russell Peck, a contemporary composer. He wrote this work in 1976 and it was a revolutionary story piece for narrator and orchestra.

To advertise the concert, I rented a Mother Goose costume and rustled up Jack and Jill costumes for David and Deborah. At the last minute, I surprised them and took them out of school with costumes in hand. We three then went on the TV program "Bozo, the Clown" to advertise this new concert and concert series.

After working on staff with the symphony for several years, I was appointed as a board member for the Grand Rapids Symphony and served in that position for nine years. During my board time experience, I raised funds for the Youth Symphony, managed trips, and planned other youth symphony events. By this time, David was playing the cello and was a member of the youth symphony.

Recently, I ran into one of the older symphony board members and we reminisced about those early days. "Do you remember the time when there were no funds for the Youth Symphony and there was a vote on the table to discontinue it?" he recalled. "You pounded the table, said that you would give the first donation, and then pointed to each of us around the table, ordering us to individually give a donation."

In five minutes, the Youth Symphony was alive again with full funds to support it and is still a vital part of our community today. As this gentleman recalled that experience, I felt so satisfied. I had fought for youth and music.

For the second year in Grand Rapids, David and Deborah moved across the street to Mulick Park School, a public school. We tried Christian private education but found that, while there were many worthy aspects to it, for our family it wasn't a fit.

The teachers and staff were kind but our kids had a hard time fitting in with the other students. Deborah and David were "foreigners" from Canada, and in those days the Christian Reformed schools in Grand Rapids were entrenched in Dutch subculture. Our family had no relatives at the school, and we didn't attend a Christian Reformed Church either (at least not then).

We also realized that we had been subconsciously outsourcing our children's spiritual formation to the school. Maybe it was because we were paying for a Christian education, but we dropped the ball a bit on prayer and devotions at home, perhaps thinking the responsibility to disciple our children now lay with Sylvan Christian School and not us. The truth is, the teaching and modeling that goes in the home is the most important by far. We learned our lesson.

We moved the kids literally across the street to Mulick Park and this seemed like a better fit, although when Deborah read this narrative, she remembered some frustrating times of bullying and other situations which are tough for a kid. I remember this with sadness.

I wasn't as available as I would have liked to be to deal with this because I was working full time. With Steve in residency, my working was a necessity for us as a family at the time. Also they were the new kids on the block and I don't want to underestimate the adjustments that children experience with changes of country and school.

All of that said, it still was easier for them to fit in with its diverse student body, having lived in the Northwest Territories and western Canada. Our kids were accustomed to being in a mix of skin colors and cultures, and it was in this type of environment where they felt most comfortable. After graduating from Mulick Park in the eighth grade, both David and Deborah chose to go on to our local public high school, Ottawa Hills High School.

An African-American friend of David's that I met recently, remembered when he first met Dave during recess at the new school and was happy to find a "white guy" who had an afro just like him. David has always had curly hair.

Another interesting experience of changing schools to Mulick Park was our friendship with Beth Myslack. Our lives were to converge at the intersection of tragedy and redemption. Mrs. Myslack was David's third grade teacher, and we were to meet her for the first time at parent teacher conferences.

Apparently, the week before David had told the class that God still raised people from the dead! During our devotions, we as a family had being studying a book called *Like a Mighty Wind* by Mel Tari. Inside were stories of miracles, including the raising of the dead, in Indonesia.

As you can imagine, this made for some eye raising on the teacher's part. "David is doing well in his schoolwork," she said, "but I'm curious why he is telling people that God can raise people from the dead." An interesting discussion followed, and we invited Beth over for dinner to continue the conversation. David had planted a seed.

A firm friendship between Beth and I was established when tragedy struck. David's classmate and fellow crossing guard, Linda Vanderveen, was abducted from her post at the next block from David's post. She was brutally murdered in the first week of April of 1979.

The whole community was in shock, devastated, confused, and frightened. The police interviewed us all, including David They eventually did find the murderer and incarcerated him, but we endured forty-two intense days while we lived uncomfortably in the unknown. Who did this to dear Linda? Was this person going to kill another child? Were our children safe?

The next day, when David had to go to his post on the corner as a safety, we were both scared. David and I talked about the fact that we were not going to let fear rule our lives. We prayed and then I walked to his corner with my son and stayed with him for the rest of his duty.

Linda's fellow classmates and their parents all attended her funeral, but of course there was little finality or peace to be had at the funeral of a murdered eleven-year-old girl. The heinous nature of her death haunted everyone, especially her classmates at Mulick Park. Beth as a teacher at the school watched and listened as families attempted to process this horrific event in their lives.

People said unhelpful things as they tried to make sense of what was senseless on a human level. "God must have wanted Linda in Heaven," one person said to Beth. "He needed another angel." Or, "This must have been what was best for the Vanderveen family."

This was absolute nonsense, and we were able to help Beth sort out these comments in light of a Christian worldview, which recognizes the presence of evil in our environment. Linda's murder was evil, and it was perpetrated by the evil one. God wept at this tragedy and was close by the suffering family, never leaving their sides.

There was a redemptive piece that came from this tragedy. For us, one redemptive thing was Beth receiving Jesus as her Savior: a God-made miracle amid a man-made heartbreak. This is definitely not to say one event equals out the other. I can't imagine anything more tragic than losing a child—especially a child who was tragically murdered.

Beth recently called me and thanked me for sharing the Gospel with her in 1979. She was asked by her church to give her testimony of almost forty years of following Jesus. "Thank you for staying with me as a baby Christian and helping me grow," she said. From that first seed planted by a child speaking faith in his classroom, Beth led others to Jesus, including her husband, mother, children, and some extended family.

Family Vignettes (as I remember them)

Cakes: Deborah's annual birthday cake was a rag doll cake decorated with white, gooey icing, multi-colored sprinkles, and red and black string licorice. "Suzy" came alive at the table when I carefully placed her gum drop heart over her apron and she greeted the little birthday guests in her Suzy voice.

This Suzy cake continued even when Deb was married. Once, when her girlfriend Jenny flew out to visit Deb for her birthday, I sent a miniature Suzy cake on the plane with her.

David's cake was "Gerry Giraffe," featuring at least two feet of neck covered with yellow icing, chocolate spots, and black licorice eyelashes. When he got too old for "Gerry Giraffe," I made a Detroit Tigers baseball boy cake, and then a guitar cake when he was in college. Guess who was having the most fun with these cakes? I'm not sure if it mattered much to the birthday boy and girl, but it was sure much fun for me.

Vacations: One year we bought an old camper truck. We drove it out west to Banff to visit our friends there. This mode of travel was much better than our old laborious car trips across Canada to visit family in Toronto. We stocked the little camper kitchen and refrigerator with good healthy food and snacks.

In the past, on our car trips, we experienced some friction when Steve wanted to keep going and he gave us all grief if we had to stop for human needs like the bathroom or food. He could go long distances without either. Does that sound like a lot of men you know? So with this camper that problem was solved.

Steve would get up early to make distance for a couple of hours while we were still asleep. That fit us all since he was an early riser and I am not. He'd stop after a few hours at a picnic spot, and the kids and I would arise, make coffee, bacon, and eggs on our Coleman stove. Yum! Nothing tastes better than eating in the outdoors. Well rested and fed, I would take over the driving for the next few hours.

Pets: Pets always have a way of making a house feel like a home. We had enjoyed having kittens, Sam and Spring (a stray abandoned kitten we rescued from under our house while living in Banff). When we left Banff these two cats were adopted into loving homes. So we wanted another kitten when we arrived in Grand Rapids.

Two strays seemed to adopt us, probably because we kept putting food out. We ended up adopting one of the stray kittens, Pumpkin, who became our beloved pet for eighteen years. Good old Pumpkin (whom I've already told you about in my "cat miracles" stories) thought she was a dog, showering us with affection and following us through the snow as we walked to the skating rink at Mulick Park. She would wait for us to skate and then follow us back home.

One night, I remember waking up and thinking, "What's the neighbor doing running a tractor in the middle of the night?" When I opened my eyes, I saw Pumpkin with her paw placed ever so gently on my cheek, purring like a motor and lovingly gazing at me, wanting me to wake up.

Matching Outfits: The first church we attended in Grand Rapids was the Drive-In Church, located at a movie theater at the corner of East Beltline and 28th Street. What a novelty, we thought. We met some folks there who invited us to Fifth Reformed, since Drive-In Church was one of their ministries. After attending Christ Church briefly, we settled into Fifth Reformed, which had a great program for teenagers.

Sometimes, at the Drive-In church we played music together and even performed in matching outfits of jeans and Izod green/navy striped shirts. We really should have billed ourselves the "Van King Family Singers." But then again, maybe not. These interludes of family togetherness ground to a halt once David and Deborah became teenagers. Mysteriously, they suddenly didn't want to be seen wearing matching outfits with their parents.

Somehow this family sing-along business became less awkward and more acceptable when they were in their college years. At that point, the "Van King Family Singers" even included a few of their college friends, brought home for the holidays.

Argo Night: When the children were a bit older, we held "Argo Night" on Sunday nights. This was to encourage our family to row together like the Argonauts of old. It was also a tip of the hat to our hometown football team, the Toronto Argonauts of the Canadian Football League. Steve came up with this unique name.

During this family meeting, we would enjoy some special food, such as egg rolls, fancy sandwiches in the shape of cellos or soccer balls, and sit in front of an open fire, discussing an issue and praying together. Each member of the family had a notebook in which we would write a question for the week: What do you like/not like about our family? What are your hopes for this vacation? Christmas? Trip? What went wrong for you last week? What went right?

One Argo Night the topic was forgiveness. The kids were upset that they had not been invited to a cousin's wedding in Toronto, even though both Steve and I were participating in the wedding. After all, the kids would have to be joining us on the trip. We could hardly leave them at home! I privately felt that the least the cousin could do was invite our children to the wedding also, but it was out of my control.

We were hashing this out, accepting their feelings and trying to come to a resolution of some kind. "Let's pray about it," I said. "I think we all need to forgive because I'm upset too." We talked more and prayed.

Ring … Ring … Ring. The couple phoned to say that they'd had some cancellations and that our kids were now invited to the wedding. This was an immediate answer to prayer and great fun. Yes, God does see our hearts and blesses us when we follow his Word.

I remember many good family times in Grand Rapids where most of our social life as parents was attending swim meets, hockey games, youth symphony. It was fun for me to host Young Life meetings in our large family room downstairs, as well as hospital parties, church parties, and the annual parties for our kid's swim and hockey get-togethers.

As the children matured, I was anticipating the time when they would be "flying the coup" and I would have time on my hands. No big parties to plan and enjoy. At least I had my love of music to keep me occupied

Christmas: Having moved to Grand Rapids we were now within driving distance of our Toronto families. This was definitely an advantage for us. It meant we could have many Christmas celebrations together. One time the whole White family and Gramma and Grampa King came for Christmas. Mary Ellen was only one year old so that's quite a few years ago.

I remember that we had fun over the days of Christmas with the Secret Santas! Everyone trying to fool the rest and keep the secrets of who was their secret Santa. We also hosted the Greens and the Wilson families and it was wonderful being close enough for that to happen. One summer we practiced a string quartet with Deb (violin,) Dave (cello), and cousins Judy and Jill (violin). These beautiful teenagers together ministered to my mamma's heart.

Another Christmas Eve I had instituted the tradition of a secret dinner in a gift wrapped box under the Christmas tree. I'd secretly fill the boxes with special food and treats and gather the family around the tree around dinner time and say, "I've been too tired to make supper tonight." But you could open one of your presents!

This joke worked for the first time with surprised delight from the children. After that when we did the same thing for years after, we pretended but it was still fun. And Deborah for a few years continued the tradition with her family.

One year when the kids were teenagers we drove to Florida to Disney World for Christmas with some friends. It was lovely watching the sea lions do their dancing routines through the sunlit glistening waves as we sat at a beachside hotel enjoying a Christmas Dinner.

Another time in Grand Rapids we had a French Christmas Eve, with French invitations, Tourtier, a Yule log desert, and French Christmas Carols around the piano.

When the kids were younger, probably in the Banff years, I tried to have Dave and Deb dress up as Mary and Joseph and we would read the Christmas story as they acted it out. I have vivid pictures of them in their PJs.

Fast forward to a Christmas Eve forty years later that I am remembering: I produced (please take that word tongue-in-cheek) another Christmas Eve pageant with the grandkids, all 7 of them. We spent the afternoon making costumes, cutting up paper for hay in the doll cradle, and all the kids seven years old and under participated.

Since Caleb who played the King, was old enough to read, he practiced with a little script that I had written. Lilly, still a baby, played baby Jesus. Parker was Joseph, and Campbell was Mary. Oh, how cute they looked. Shelby and Maddie were sweet angels with glittery ropes as halos, and Alex was a shepherd, staff and all.

We had shepherds and kings, all dressed up from my dress-up trunk, to impress. I found some photos recently of this production and fondly reminisced.

I remember it being total bedlam as this acting troupe walked out of my bedroom to an audience of their two sets of parents seated on the sofa in the living room. I think the parents thought that I was crazy. Maybe I am, but for me that was fun.

I enjoyed Christmas and still do, although the participants have changed drastically. I usually travel to Deb and Kent's home for Christmas now that I'm alone. I love being with the family. I miss those early days when I would have everyone home together.

Biking, ice skating, and cross-country skiing together

In winter we enjoyed ice skating and cross-country skiing together, while warmer months found us swimming together in our pool. Also we all enjoyed biking together.

One year we had an adventure with another family on a three-day organized biking trip up to Ludington, MI. The schedule, the meals, and accommodation had all been arranged by the touring company; all we had to do was ride the bikes. I remember one of the leaders coming back for me as I struggled up a loooong hill as he gave me a little push. Of course, the rest of the family was far ahead.

Canadian Festival of Youth Orchestra (CFYO)

For ten years I had the opportunity to work as the Music Coordinator for the Canadian Festival of Youth Orchestras. This job began when we were still in Banff and I was hired for this position by the Banff School of Fine Arts.

When we moved to Grand Rapids, I continued with this job and travelled back and forth to Banff, Alberta, for the Festival every two years. The Festival consisted of a youth orchestra from each of the Canadian Provinces traveling to Banff and participating in a ten-day orchestra and master class experience culminating in a concert by each of the orchestras, which were conducted by a famous Canadian conductor.

It was an amazing and enjoyable experience for me, and certainly one that caused me to grow both professionally and personally. During one of those festivals, the family joined me to downhill ski on the rugged snow-clad mountains in Banff National Park.

***

Graduate School

After ten years in the music business, I decided to go to graduate school for my Master of Social Work degree. Two years beforehand, I had desperately wanted to go to graduate school with a friend of mine. Steve balked—he was still in residency training and couldn't handle the extra pressure of me also studying. So reluctantly, very reluctantly, I agreed to put it off.

When Steve was finished with his training, he gladly concurred I should study. "I'm willing to clean bathrooms," he said, cheerfully. The first graduate program I had so badly wanted to attend had actually lost its accreditation and my friend didn't even get her degree. God knew what was best for me and used my husband in that process.

I had always had a bent and a desire to minister to people in distress. I wanted a professional degree so I could have something substantial to do with my time once my children left home. I loved the reading and the studying, which I did during the day, and attended graduate school in Grand Rapids three nights a week.

I had the best of both worlds because I didn't need to make a living during the day like most of my classmates. I made supper before leaving at 5:30 p.m., and then Steve ate with the kids. I was home just after 9 p.m.

David and Deborah were attending high school by then, and I had embarked on a new and fulfilling vocational path. The kids were growing up, and we all were planting deep roots in West Michigan soil. By this time we had decided to stay in Grand Rapids and Steve had successfully completed his board certifications as a Psychiatrist.

Musing

It's amazing to me how God's timing and his provisions are right on. Thank you, Lord, for your faithfulness and for leading us.

Chapter 15

Holding on in a Different Way

Fixing our eyes on Jesus, the pioneer and perfecter of faith. For the joy set before him he endured the cross, scorning its shame, and sat down at the right hand of the throne of God. Consider him who endured such opposition from sinners, *so that you will not grow weary and lose heart* (Hebrews 12:2,3). [Italics mine]

After eight years on Griggs Street, we wanted to move to a larger home. Our cozy first residence in Grand Rapids was quaint, but there wasn't enough space for David and Deborah to entertain their friends. That was important to us. I loved for the children to bring their friends home.

We looked all around the neighborhood for another house, and it wasn't long until we found a property on Breton Road, still in the same school district and neighborhood. We wanted the kids to stay in the same school.

Before long we had a buyer for our Griggs home and we had purchased the ranch house with a downstairs walk-out patio. I also had to be sure that my grand piano could find its home there. Another move, but a good one.

Our Breton home, on its over two acres of wooded land with a ravine, had five bedrooms, three full bathrooms, and a very large family room. In addition, it had an amazing space over the double garage with a separate entrance, which we used as a counseling office for all the years that we lived there.

As a mom, I truly enjoyed the teenage years with my two children.

Between hockey games, swim meets, soccer games, youth symphony, youth choir at church, school orchestra and quartets, not to mention all the friends coming and going, I was in my element. The more the merrier for me!

Steve and I would scream our heads off during Deborah's swim meets. Eventually, she came in first in the city of Grand Rapids for "The Fly." We also screamed at David's hockey games. David used to get teased when he showed up for hockey practice after youth symphony carrying his cello, as well as all of his hockey equipment.

Steve was the team doctor for the hockey team, and we both enjoyed the hockey games as loyal Canadians, our cheers reverberating off the lofty ceiling of the Jolly Roger Ice Arena.

Our social life centered around attending as many of David and Deborah's events as we could, or else hosting parties and events in our home. Large groups of kids gathered in our spacious downstairs family room for Young Life meetings. We hosted the annual hospital parties, the hockey/parent parties, the swim team parties and mission committee/elder parties from church since we were both very involved at our church as well.

Both Dave and Deb attended Ottawa Hills High School. Neither one of my children was difficult to raise although we as a family experienced our share of the usual ups and downs. We didn't allow MTV or R rated movies at our house.

Of course, the response to that was the boilerplate response of teenagers everywhere: "Well, I could watch that stuff at my friend's house!"

To which my reply was usually: "If you do watch that program or movie or music video over there, then it's your responsibility, not mine."

We tried to limit TV using a "ticket system" when they had been in elementary school. For every half hour David or Deborah read a book, they could watch a half hour of TV. Fast forward to my grandkids and their media intake. I once overheard Lilly, then four, saying to Alex, six, "We can't watch that, Alex. It is inappropriate."

Of course, that comment was overheard before all the grandchildren (and children everywhere) had iPhones and iPads, amounting to the same thing as individual televisions and movie theaters. Now limiting phones and tablets and screen time is a different story and an incredible challenge for today's parents. I don't envy them!

We made many mistakes. Many times, I told my oldest child, "I've never had a sixteen-year-old before. You are going to have tell me what you need." And even then, I didn't always get it. David came in the door from school one day and I immediately began barking orders like a drill sergeant. "OK. You need to practice your cello! And then do your homework."

It certainly wasn't the most loving way to greet someone I loved after a hard day at school. "I was going to do it, but now I don't want to," he replied, quite annoyed. "You didn't even say 'Hello, how was your day?'" Ugh!

Live and learn, moms. So sometimes I'd say, "Sorry, let's re-run that tape" and David would back out the door and "come home" again.

Since David and Deborah were close in age, they participated in a lot of the same activities, and sometimes hung out together with the same friends. Of course, Deb wishes that she had a sister as well, and I do too. At least she has Kent's sisters, to whom she is close.

It's always helpful to have a sibling, whether a brother or a sister, who has experienced the same growing up experiences and the same parents. Together, they can complain and throw their parents under the bus, which I think my children still do. I used to throw my own parents under the bus with my sisters, so I can't complain, can I?

As parents, Steve and I were quite different, especially when it came to finances. My husband's parents had grown up in the Depression and money was very tight. Steve, according to his report, was largely responsible for his own clothing and entertainment from the time he was twelve years old.

He worked on paper routes, delivered pharmacy orders and fish and chips around the neighborhood on his bicycle, and was able to save quite a bit of money from his cobbled jobs. He sure was enterprising and a hard worker.

Steve King could never be accused of being a spender. He was strict in terms of the children's work ethic and money management. Steve was especially hard on David and made him work all through high school and got him shifts as an orderly at the hospital when he was in college. I wish that I could undo that because looking back, it seemed like too much work for a college student.

The upside is that David is a very good manager of his finances and he had no debts when he finished college. I wrote a note to David recently about his dad being hard on him. Here is David's email response:

> Thanks Mom - I agree that Dad was a "tight wad" but I think the lessons he taught me were more beneficial than harmful. He was harder on me than Deb but I am also harder on myself. The biggest lesson that he taught me about finances was that you cannot out give God.
> This has been the basis for my finances and I believe that my family is blessed because of that lesson. I'm not scarred because of his cheapness! I remember those things but more because they represent characteristics of Dad. I joke with you about it because I get a reaction and because it's fun to think about some of Dad's crazy nuances.
> I am the man I am today because of the Old Fella! He was a good father to me despite his flaws. I hope my kids will say the same thing about me some day. I appreciate the thoughts but it's really not a deep scar. Thanks, though!

My response to that email?

> You're right Dave. You have become an amazing father to your children and a good provider.

By the time Deborah needed money, Steve was softening in this area. But he still erred on the side of not spoiling her. One time I remember her fixing the tail pipe of her old car with a Coke can, before leaving home to drive back to college at Wheaton. I really don't know how I allowed her to travel in such a rickety car, but I suppose it seemed okay at the time.

In our family, money had to be earned in some way, so I would sneak Deb a $20 bill on her way out the door to go back to Wheaton. Probably because he had made a big deal out of thrifty practices, Steve also felt that he needed to secretly slip her $20.

Neither one of us let on that the other had snuck our daughter some cash, and Deb, being a smart girl, did not let on. She just took the $40 and blazed a trail to Wheaton College, probably marveling all the way! This has become a rather open family joke now, passed on to the next generation. Just yesterday, our grandson, Alex, brought it up at lunch.

Steve and I were opposites in finances and in so many other ways but we realized early on that we could bring a needed balance to each other. I felt I could give the bank away, and Steve wanted to keep the bank! When we were to travel in impoverished Liberia, Steve and I made a pact beforehand that I wouldn't give any money away unless we conferred and both agreed. So we were a protection for each other, and I'm thankful for that.

In terms of our parenting styles, Steve said that he didn't need to have any emotions because I had them all! I bubble over with emotions and easily express them, while Steve felt very limited in feeling and expressing his emotions. This disparity in our emotional articulations was probably difficult for our children. David and Deborah would come home after school and unburden all their problems on Mom.

When it was suppertime and I would ask them to unburden to Dad, often, they couldn't remember. Meanwhile, I was a basket case, a receptacle for all my children's teenage burdens, issues, and tensions. I soon realized that they just needed to unburden and then it was gone. If Dad had been at home first, they would have done the same to him.

***

Parenting and life itself presents many opportunities to offer empathy and compassion. There were tragedies during the teen years, which required our full attention as parents to help our kids get through to the other side.

Two of David and Deborah's friends died during the high school years, one from a car accident, and another by suicide. Many tears were shed during painful, wrenching, and ultimately, I hope, comforting conversations between us and them as we processed these losses together. I so wished my children hadn't had to experience those traumatic losses at such a young age.

Hopefully, I was a "good enough" mother. Early in graduate school I had taken a psychopathology class, which convinced me I had totally messed up my children, my husband, and myself! Thankfully, another class taught me about the concept of "good enough" and avoiding the high-pressure goal of perfection for the gentler "good enough" paradigm.

"Good enough," I realized, largely meant loving our children to the best of our abilities. And I believe Steve and I did. We made our fair share of mistakes like every parent. When issues from the past arise, I still try to apologize with the goal of repairing and restoring. When I look at my adult children now—including their spouses—and witness how well they have loved their own children, I am grateful.

My seven grandchildren have been loved well, and I am very proud of how they are turning out. When I tell that to Deborah she says, "Well, the jury's still out." True, but these children have had a great foundation of faith and love from both parents and that is very evident to me. How blessed I am!

***

When your children grow up and move away from home, it's a difficult, emotional process for some parents. At least it was for me. You raise your children to be independent and successful, but nonetheless it is shocking when the time comes to let them go.

Yes, you want them to achieve their goals and dreams. It's exhilarating to witness their excitement. But things are undoubtedly changing for you as a parent. You must learn to, as one therapist once told me, "hold on in a different kind of way."

When David left for college it was a major adjustment for us. Our first child was leaving the nest! For months, Steve was depressed, missing his buddy, only forty-five minutes away at Hope College in Holland, but nonetheless, no longer home.

Just one year later, Deborah left us with an empty nest. My girl and I cried almost all the way to Wheaton College, with the three of us—Steve, myself and Deborah—sitting in the front seat because the back seat and trunk were packed to the gills with her stuff. I wish I had been braver, but it was wrenching for me to let go.

So my Deborah was on her way to being grown up. Raising your children to be independent means success. Deborah was going farther away than Holland, MI, to Wheaton College in Illinois, but she had her wings and was able to fly away from the nest quite successfully.

This was a difficult transition for me, even though I now had my career—for which I am thankful. I have counseled a lot of women and have told them to give grace to themselves through this transition time. I know that it was hard for Deborah when her oldest daughter, Campbell, went off to college.

A text which I wrote her at the time was: "You have a beautiful daughter inside and out, and so do I." I was learning to let go and to "hold on in a different way."

Later, when Deborah was emancipating and getting ready for her wedding to Kent (and preparing to leave our home forever), I rode my stationary bike and listened to praise music while I exercised away my angst. Praising God even in my anxiety and loss helped me circle back to Jesus. He would be with me as I did the hard work of releasing my children and more importantly He would be with them.

Again the prayer, *"Jesus, please help me."*

Having your little duckies under the umbrella of your wings was a safe feeling. It was so comforting to know as we let go of the controls, we can place them safely under God's protection.

One chapter was closing, one of the most significant and formative stages of my life, their lives, and the life of our family—parenting my children at home. Just like every other parent before or after me, I had to remember that Jesus would be with Steve and me in the new chapters to come and more importantly, He would be with them as we loosened our grip on them.

Musing

"Jesus, Help Me."

Chapter 16

The Woman in the Coffin

By His wounds we are healed (Isaiah 53:5).

We were empty nesters, and it was time to have some more adventures. All along during the previous years, we had traveled together, going on mission trips and other ministry opportunities, mostly happy to be learning and ministering together.

Well, there was that one incident at the Grand Rapids airport, on the way to Florida ... I can't really say Steve enjoyed my company overmuch, at least not at the beginning of the trip. Let's just say I refer to this event as "The Incident Where I Was Almost Jailed and Steve Almost Divorced Me."

Before the Christian Medical Association closed in 2007 we both attended their annual meetings, serving by speaking, praying for others, and leading worship. I often led worship from the piano and played my violin in the "doctor ensembles" we put together of musical doctors in attendance. Dr. Bill Reed and I strolled around during banquets, playing our fiddles and having so much fun.

It was on our way to one of these conventions when "The Incident" happened. This was in the late eighties, long before there were heightened security checkpoints. However, I still managed to breach the security that did exist.

It was very early in the morning when we got to the airport to catch our flight to Florida, and I was excited and bubbling about this trip. Sometimes I'm bubbly when I'm excited—what can I say? Well, I said the exact wrong thing to the Transportation Security Administration. I was carrying my violin in its case when a security officer asked me what was in it.

"A machine gun," I said, with what I thought was obvious sarcasm and a bright twinkle in my eye. I mean, anybody could see that it was a violin case! Unfortunately, this officer didn't get my sense of humor. All hell broke loose at the security station—a measure of hell, anyway. I sobered up in a flash from my giddiness.

"You could have been sent to jail and fined thousands of dollars just for saying that you were carrying a machine gun!" The humorless officer berated me for some time after quickly opening my violin case to reveal … a violin.

Steve was terribly embarrassed and irritated with me. I was sure he would divorce me on the spot.

I certainly learned my lesson. On many subsequent trips to Florida with my violin, if anyone asked me what was in the case, I solemnly and with no twinkle in my eye replied that it was a violin. I didn't even add "obviously."

So often we don't open our eyes to the incredible ways God intersects with our lives. Following are a few more of the amazing ways Steve and I saw God at work in his world.

Russia and Siberia, 1990

God's light sometimes shines brightest in the most unlikely of places. Take Siberia, for example, which is not as bad as people think. It's sunny—though cold—in the winter, and in Irkutsk, where we visited, the river embankment is lined with stunning old churches with golden onion domes.

Plus, Lake Baikal, one of the world's largest, deepest, and clearest lakes, is so beautiful it will take your breath away. Beautiful, yes, but if you visited the Soviet Union before the iron curtain fell, you felt the bleakness of a people oppressed and believers persecuted.

Steve and I traveled to Siberia in 1990, just before the Berlin Wall came down. We were there to present papers at a University medical conference about the Care of the Geriatric Population at the University of Irkutsk. Steve's paper was on Depression in the Elderly, and mine was on Substance Abuse in the Elderly, both escalating issues. I also wanted to mention AA treatment, so I could talk about a "Higher Power." Both of our papers were translated into Russian.

First, we had to get to Russia, and then board a plane in Moscow—a scary proposition in those days. While in Moscow, we were treated to an underground art display in the basement of an old building. The paintings had been rescued from the Russian Revolution and two world wars and hidden away. As an art lover, viewing this secret art was a phenomenal opportunity.

We enjoyed certain aspects of Russia, but this was still the cold war, and we were in enemy territory. We had been so anxious about this trip because of the distance and the danger involved. Our prayer was "*Lord, if this is not your will then close all the doors.*" This brought us spiritual peace, but as we were about to get on a rickety looking airplane for an eight-hour flight from Moscow to Siberia, our very human fears rose to the surface.

"I guess we're going," I said to Steve as we locked wide eyes right before boarding. Part of me wanted to bolt, especially after getting on the airplane, with its buzzing flies, open flapping overhead compartments and smells of garlic and whatever else wafting around us. And then we were on our way, buckled in to Lord knows what. *Lord, please see us through and be near to us on this horrible airplane!* I prayed silently.

I was seated next to a large man the whole eight-hour trip. He was none too friendly, wore a mysterious black fedora pulled over his face and held on to a large briefcase on his lap the entire time. I imagined that he was a spy or a criminal and that his suitcase was full of money. This did not soothe my nerves. Oh dear, my imagination again.

Once we touched down in Irkutsk, my breathing relaxed. God had carried us safely thus far and He would carry us through our entire assignment. Despite the harrowing flight, our Siberian hosts were lovely. They treated us with utmost hospitality and warmth, seeing to every one of our needs.

I still cherish their gifts to me, a beautiful wool scarf (which our hosts asked me to choose from a selection, probably obtained off the black market), and a samovar. When we ducked into the shops to look around, most of the shelves were bare. There were hardly any goods available and the barrenness was shocking.

When we later returned to Grand Rapids, I walked in to our local D&W food market, stocked to the brim with every color and shape of gorgeous produce, every shelf stocked to capacity. I started to cry, unable to wrap my mind around the incongruence of Siberia's empty, darkened shelves compared to America's abundance. How could one keep both pictures in the same head?

When Steve and I presented the medical papers at the conference, a doctor in the audience asked about my faith. I had mentioned God as a higher power in my portion of the talk. "Could you tell us what you believe"?

When I explained that I was a Christian, he asked me to explain what that meant. This line of questioning happened during the question and answer time. It was a perfect setup to share the gospel of Christ. Imagine that—an opportunity to be an evangelist during a Communist medical conference!

Later, this same gentleman asked us to pray for him through an interpreter. He used hand motions to convey a gun to his head, communicating that his grandfather, an orthodox priest, had been murdered for his beliefs. Though secret and even dangerous to believe in Jesus during those years, the man obviously harbored a genuine faith. While I spoke, the Holy Spirit revealed to him I was a like spirit.

Steve and I had brought a suitcase of Bibles with us to Siberia, thinking we would give them to the local church. The doctors we met at the conference had no Bibles, and we ended up giving them all away right there. God knew who those Bibles were for all along.

There was a banquet while we were there, with hearty Slavic fare and vodka flowing freely. Tall and handsome Andrei, one of the doctors from the conference whom I believed to be a secret Christian, got up and gave a speech.

"Thank you for coming, dear Americans with the light in your eyes." Wow! That was you, Holy Spirit. The light in our eyes was you!

I'll never forget another memory from that same banquet. A tall, husky Siberian woman came up to Steve quite eagerly. "I vant to daaanse with ya, Dr. King," she stated bluntly as she pulled a panic-stricken Steve to the dance floor. Oh, if you could have seen the look on his face! He really didn't know how to dance and could be quite shy. Dr. King survived the experience and we laughed together afterwards.

The next day we were invited to an outdoor picnic on the banks of the beautiful Lake Baikal to celebrate with a group of Siberian doctors from the conference. Surrounded by mile-high snowcapped mountains, the deep blues and greens of the lake called to us as we mingled with our new doctor friends and enjoyed their Russian treats.

The previous day at the conference, another doctor named Dimitri had approached us with a request. "Could I get a Bible for my wife, Arisha?" he asked. "She has only ever dreamed of having a Bible." Of course, we gladly gave him one.

When we arrived at our outdoor party, Arisha, Dimitri's wife ran up to me. "Thank you for the Bible," Arisha said. "Do you know God? Can you tell me how I know God, too?" She knew some English and I did not know any Russian.

"Oh yes," I said. Using hand motions, I said, "God is up there, and we are down here. The way we get to God is through Jesus who died on the cross. For our sins." And I drew a cross in the air. Then I drew a heart in the sand with a door in the center of the heart. "Jesus knocks on this door and if we open the door, say we are sorry for our sins, and ask him to come in, He will," I said.

She looked at me with tears in her eyes. The Holy Spirit was working. "I like to do that now, please." It was with this simple outline of the Gospel message that I led Arisha in a prayer to repent of her sins and accept Jesus as her Savior.

We both were crying and hugging. Steve who was standing further up the bank snapped a photo. Somehow, it seemed too simple. *Did this really happen*? I wondered.

For a couple of years, Arisha wrote me letters about how the light had come on in her life for the first time. I shared more Scripture verses with her to look up in her Russian Bible, as I realized that the miracle of salvation had occurred on that beautiful riverbank on the other side of the world.

Germany, Poland, Romania, Belarus—2001

Before going on a multi-week ministry trip to Europe and the former Soviet Union, we had asked for prayer from our church. We were part of a team from Christ for the Nations, including my friend and mentor, Freda Lindsay. During that prayer, one of the young women praying had a vision of a woman in a coffin.

I also saw this woman's face in my spirit. I can't really describe what she looked like. I just knew that I would be able to recognize her because of this Holy Spirit vision. During the whole trip, I looked for this woman's face in the faces of the many people we encountered. *I wonder what that woman's face is all about*, I thought more than once.

We prayed for many people throughout our meetings as we visited Bible schools and churches. God also ministered to us, reaching deep into Steve's soul to heal him of a long-buried wound. In Germany, Steve was confronted with the fact that he had borne a lifelong grievance against the country that "stole" his father for the first two years of Steve's life.

Steve's father had enlisted and served overseas during World War II. This wasn't a conscious thought going into the trip, but as he spoke up at the podium in Frankfurt, Steve got in touch with those early memories of deprivation. He hadn't realized how deprived of his father he had felt as a baby and toddler, how abandoned. In the early months of Steve's infancy, he had been very sick with a "failure to thrive" syndrome.

Maybe this had something to do with his father exiting the family to go to war when Steve was in utero, leading to his mother's crippling depression. For much of those two years, his mother had not known if her husband was alive or dead. And now all at once, my husband experienced profound spiritual healing and forgiveness for Germany.

Steve's father, a Scot named James King, was a fourteen-year-old immigrant, with only an 8th grade education. One of sixteen children, he lived with his two older sisters in Canada, going to work immediately to support the sister who was a widow.

Years later when James married Evelyn (Steve's mother), he enlisted in WWII, hoping to gain some credibility from his staunch English father-in-law. In fact, Steve's brother, Gord, who was ten years old at the time, was the only one who accompanied James to see him off to war. Evelyn was pregnant with Steve at that time and had a lot of sickness.

Upon returning from the war, James became educated as an electrician and worked diligently, providing a good stable income for his family. This precious couple, Jim and Evelyn, with limited education became the parents of a veterinarian and PhD researcher, a teacher, and my husband, a medical doctor and board-certified psychiatrist. And my in-laws were simply the best grandparents who ever lived.

Back in Europe on our trip, it was a powerful moment when Steve accessed those early, painful memories of an absent father and a mother in the clutches of depression. He had repressed these memories, hidden far beneath the surface of his consciousness, and now God had brought those memories up to bind and heal them. How remarkable that God brought Steve into the presence of his enemies, so to speak, to do his healing work!

Later that year, when we were in Jamaica at the Christ for the Nations School there, Steve was asked to speak in place of Benny Hinn who had been detained. Imagine that! But I already told you that Sister Lindsay had such an affection and soft spot for Steve. He had deeply ministered to her after her husband's death.

Steve broke down in tears from the platform as he was speaking of this experience in Germany. Since he couldn't seem to stop his weeping, I walked up to the stage to help him, taking over his message, as he could not continue speaking. It turned out to be a mighty, healing time as we prayed for many people after his outpouring of emotion—an extremely rare experience for Steve.

The entire European trip was a conduit of power, healing, and love. Several memories shine, such as the Sunday in Gdansk, Poland. Steve had preached the Sunday morning sermon in an old church. (By "old" I mean some of these grand churches in Gdansk had been built in the 1300-1500s, and featured spectacular domes, pipe organs, and ancient crypts.)

Afterward we had lunch in an old nightclub with a beautiful grand piano. I couldn't resist playing the piano and asked Sister Lindsay to join me in singing a worship song set to *O Sole Mio*. Beautiful! And so much fun for me.

***

Remember the woman in the coffin? Sort of hard to forget her! That piece of the story brings us to Belarus, a landlocked country in Eastern Europe bordered by Russia to the northeast, Ukraine to the south, Poland to the west, and Lithuania and Latvia to the northwest.

Heavily forested Belarus became a republic on July 27, 1990, eleven years before our trip. The country has been labeled "Europe's last dictatorship" by some Western journalists, and indeed we noticed a heaviness and darkness there. These precious people had been oppressed for so long under the Soviet regime.

On our first day in Belarus, we traveled to a sanatorium, a medical facility most typically associated with treatment of tuberculosis, located in a remote wooded village. Belarus represents the highest proportion of multi-drug resistant Tuberculosis ever recorded in the world. We were on a mission—me reluctantly—to find and pray with the bride of one of the Bible school teachers we had met. She was a patient at the facility.

Earlier, Steve and I had been at a pastor's luncheon at the Bible College and sat beside a young pastor missionary from Canada. He told us his story of marrying his Belarusian bride six months before, and why they could not be together now. Katya, like so many others in her country, had contracted Tuberculosis and had been sent to live in a sanitarium for several months. Of course, the young pastor was deeply troubled about his wife.

"Has anyone gone with you to the sanitarium to pray for her and anoint her with oil?" I heard Steve ask him. *Uh oh*, I thought.

"No," the young pastor said. "Katya is contagious, and people are afraid to go in case they might catch TB. But I do visit her anyway," he added.

"When are you going again?" Steve again. *Gulp*.

"This afternoon," he replied. Oh boy … I could see where my afternoon was headed, and it was nowhere I wanted to go. I had my plans for the afternoon all figured out: preparation for my teaching that evening.

The Canadian pastor eagerly agreed when Steve asked if we could go with him to the sanitarium and pray for Katya. *What a crazy idea!* I thought. *Steve! What have you gotten us into this time?* I went (inwardly) kicking and screaming, but before we left we asked for prayer from the CFNI team. Freda Lindsay had herself been healed of TB and had a special anointing and feeling for its victims.

The sanatorium was a few hours' drive away, so I had time to sort out my feelings in the back seat of a 1980s era Skoda. One part of me was annoyed, most of all about the fact that now I would have no time to prepare for my evening message at the Bible college. But the other, more sanctified, part of me silently confessed my resistance and tried to surrender the whole thing to the Lord.

I thought about the woman in the coffin. Over the weeks of ministering in other countries and praying healing for many dear folks in long lines, I had yet to "see" her face. What was that all about?

Upon arriving at the sanatorium, I felt such darkness in my spirit that I didn't even want to get out of the car. Fighting the nausea that curdled my stomach, I took a deep breath and got out of the car. Past experience had taught me to pray during times of sudden darkness, spiritual warfare prayers, to see what God wanted me to do. I prayed the mind of Christ, because my mind was screaming to get out of there.

Steve and I and the young Canadian pastor entered the sanitarium, a dark, depressing Soviet era building, and a warehouse for the sick and forgotten. A person at the front desk called for Katya. Presently a lovely young woman came into the lobby to meet us. *And …*

Katya's face was the face of the lady in the coffin. I knew in that moment God wanted me exactly where I was, standing in a gloomy cinder block structure in the forests of Belarus, an ambassador of his hope because this was a place where hope was in short supply. I could feel the heaviness in my bones.

We prayed immediately, standing there in the lobby. I rested my hand on Katya and the Lord gave me a "word of knowledge," a picture of a little girl who had been abused.

"Katya," I said gently, explaining my mental picture, "does this mean anything to you?"

She began to cry, her hidden wound brought to the surface to be healed. Indeed, Katya was instantly healed of this memory. We then took her to a quiet place on the ward to pray.

Walking around the sanitarium, I noticed the strong chemical smell of disinfectant infusing the atmosphere. The facility was dark and overcrowded, with six to eight beds in a room. My heart ached for this priceless child of God, stuck in such a horrible place. We laid hands on her, anointed her with oil, and prayed to our mighty God that Katya would be healed of tuberculosis.

We drove back to the Bible school in Minsk, knowing that God was at work in Katya's life somehow and trusting him for the outcome. All we can do is be obedient to his assignments, move forward, and leave the results to him.

Remember, that night I was slated to be the speaker at the Bible College, but because of the trip to the sanitarium, I did not have time to prepare. However, God blessed my decision to obey him and go to Katya.

During worship, before I went up to the podium, I felt an incredible sense of God's presence through the music. He felt so near me as I soaked in the violin and saxophone and voices of God's people worshipping him. There was perfect shalom—nothing missing, nothing broken—as I connected to the people, the worship, and the spirit of God beyond human understanding. I felt like I was in Heaven and never wanted to leave.

Some months later, we got a letter from Belarus, from the young Canadian pastor. He rejoiced at his wife's complete healing. Not long after our visit, he had taken Katya from the sanatorium and had her checked by a doctor.

According to his report, the doctor was amazed because Katya's lungs, when X-rayed, showed no sign of the disease, not even scar tissue which can often be seen after TB. We cheered with them both in spirit and together at home.

How humbled and grateful we were to be given this divine appointment, part of a much bigger mission of God's people ministering together. It all started at our church in Grand Rapids, with that prayer vision of a woman in the coffin.

Dominican Republic, Haiti, and WYAM—1993

One of the biggest lessons we learned on our travels was to trust and obey God despite our feelings. One mission trip which drove this lesson home for me was our voyage to the Dominican Republic and Haiti on a ship called: *The Mercy Ship*.

We had applied to Youth with a Mission (YWAM) to do a short-term medical mission on one of their ships. Those ships do fantastic work and Steve and I wanted to be a part of it. According to their website, a ship is the most effective platform to deliver a state-of-the-art hospital to regions where clean water, electricity, medical facilities, and personnel is limited or nonexistent.

Because more than 50% of the world's population lives within 100 miles of the coast, medical ships can reach more people who need care. YWAM also has a strong spiritual ministry component to their work and we felt our combined skill set would dovetail perfectly with their mission.

However, when we applied, YWAM wrote us back and stated that they didn't want doctors' wives to come along on the ships because they typically treated it as a vacation. Their short-term mission trips, they said firmly, were anything but vacations. I was offended by their response.

They were lumping me in with a stereotype I disliked. By then I was a mental health professional, had written books, and spoken in venues all over the world. Yet it seemed they defined me, sight unseen, as someone who would sip fruity drinks on the promenade deck while other volunteers worked their fingers to the bone. My nose was out of joint.

Somehow, we convinced the organization that I would treat this boat ride as an opportunity to serve the Lord, not a holiday. They gave in and granted me permission to come along. Steve was immediately put to work treating patients, and I was designated to help in the laundry, and with cutting out labels in the library. Though not over-joyed with my assignment, I tried to keep surrendering my situation to the Lord, asking for help hour by hour to have a good attitude.

Jesus, help me!

I was somewhat dreading the first chapel service, because leading worship and speaking were the gifts I had to offer—gifts that were not accepted. But I went anyway, and discovered some Canadian chaplains were leading the service. *I will choose to be friendly*, I thought.

When I introduced myself, I was in for a surprise. "Oh Judy, you and Steve are here?" The chaplains, Jack and Myrna Hill were surprised and delighted. Suddenly, I recognized them, too.

Some thirty years earlier we had visited a remote island called Bella Coola off the coast of Vancouver, landing in a float plane (so much fun!) to look over a mission opportunity in a hospital there. We had spent an evening with these same chaplains, praying and encouraging them.

After this introduction they immediately put me to work, leading an anger workshop for the staff and later a marriage workshop for some of the staff couples. I also had the joy of visiting some of the surrounding villages to meet with the designated health care people. We taught them how to teach the villagers to avoid disease.

I made up a song for them to sing to the tune of "Old MacDonald," incorporating the concepts 'drink clean water,' 'cover your food,' and 'wash your hands' in Spanish. The first two lines were "Diarrhea is no fun, so listen to this song." As we left the villages to return to the ship, it was fun to hear my Dominican friends gustily singing us this jaunty song all the way up the ramp!

God honored my obedience, even though I was initially irritated and offended by YWAM's lack of recognition. My pride was wounded. And that was part of the lesson. God humbled me and brought a lot of good out of this situation. That is his specialty, bringing glory out of the mundane and good out of not-so-good.

Musing

I look back at that extraordinary trip and others and marvel at God's power helping and healing his children. *I wonder how those people are doing now?* Katya in Belarus, Arisha in Siberia, and others we met on our journeys who saw Light in our eyes and wanted to know more. *Lord Jesus, I pray for them now and others who saw your light.*

Chapter 17

The Last Sunset

I am the resurrection and the life. He that believes in me, though
he is dead, yet shall he live. And whoever believes in me will
never die. Do you believe that? ((John 11:25).

Steve loved boats. Before we bought our condo we kept a seventeen-
foot motorboat on Reed's Lake in East Grand Rapids. Steve used
to call that boat his "summer office," and later our friends nicknamed
it "The Couch."

We enjoyed that time immensely, often picnicking on the boat,
taking Deb and Dave and their friends water skiing, and watching
fireworks from the boat on July 4th. A truly wonderful memory for
us was taking Deborah on her wedding day out for breakfast on the
boat and some water skiing on Reeds Lake. What a gorgeous picture
of Deborah skiing on the glassy calm waters, sun shining exuberantly
on this beautiful lithe "ballerinistic" figure.

Unfortunately, when we bought the condo in 1999, we found our
seventeen-foot boat wasn't large enough to make boating on Lake
Michigan fun or safe. The waves were too high.

Miracle of the Lake Michigan Condo

The condo itself is another *miracle* for me. I had always desired a
place on Lake Michigan, but it seemed like a pipe dream. After
David and Deborah were launched, I would pack a picnic supper,
pick Steve up at the hospital and drive to Holland State Park where
we would swim, eat our supper, and enjoy the gorgeous sunset.

One time I looked up and saw the Spyglass Condos perched on the dunes to the north. "I want one of those," I said, tongue in cheek. I didn't really believe it would ever happen. We had looked for a cottage for years and it never seemed to work out. Besides, we didn't think we had enough money.

"I don't want to go look at cottages anymore," I told Steve. We had never bought after twenty years of looking. By then it seemed to be a hobby of Steve's, but I was tired of the disappointment.

After a few years of not looking for a place on the lake, I was having my devotions and the following scripture jumped out at me again: "He is able to do exceeding greatly above all that you could ask or think." *What are you telling me Lord?* I prayed. *That's the verse you gave me before we found our first house in Grand Rapids. Do you have another place for us?*

"There's a place for sale at Spyglass," Steve, who was reading the newspaper, said. "Do you want to go for a look?"

We went and saw what was to be our condo. It was bright and had a great view. I walked out on the deck and prayed. *What about this, Lord?* He answered me immediately. "This is my provision for you."

With some inheritance money from both of our parents, we were able to make a down payment and furnish it. In the months leading up to Steve's death he made double payments on it. There was one payment left and I took care of that right after Steve died.

Idyllic Summer Days

Together, we had marvelous summers on the lake, swimming and jumping in the waves. It brought out the playful side in us both and we always emerged refreshed and rejuvenated. On many a hot day we'd ride our bikes with our bathing suits on under our shorts, so we could go directly to the beach and jump in the water.

If we'd forgotten our suits, and we were hot enough, we'd still run into the waves to cool off, even with our clothes on. Strolling on the beach, lazing in the sun and reading, watching the boats come in from the pier—we loved it all.

When the grandkids were there, we enjoyed it even more. As a family we delighted in the beach, the pool, the state park, the playground, and the outside cookouts. What fun to play with those great kids! Steve adored being Grampa.

Sunsets were one of our favorite times together. It became a ritual each evening to sit together on the deck or the landing and view God's glorious, ever-changing masterpieces in the sky. We sat in awe witnessing the reds, pinks, peaches, and other colors embellishing the horizon.

The last sunset we watched together was a week before Steve died. We had Dave and Julie's children for a few days after the family reunion in Canada.

Steve had spent *an entire year planning this reunion* for our family. Most of the family and all of the grandchildren had never been to Niagara Falls.

He arranged accommodation for us all at the top of the Empress Hotel—what a view!—and had hand drawn on goodie bags which he provided for each of the families. We wore matching red T-shirts, enjoyed walking beneath the falls, taking a boat to the brink of the falls, visiting some shows. It was a great week.

From Niagara Falls, we ended up in Newmarket for a Briggs family reunion at the Green home. It was a wonderful reunion as Steve and Jeff grilled hamburgers and everyone visited and caught up around the pool. My sister, Barb, was the best hostess of large family gatherings that you could imagine.

There was always tons of great homemade food. She even provided crafts and activities for the younger kids to do. She was an experienced teacher and knew just what to do. What an amazing experience for the last time as a complete entire family. In fact, when Steve died, he was working on a collage of photos from that memorable reunion.

On the way home through rural Ontario we stopped at Thunder Beach, and stayed a few days on beautiful Georgian Bay at my sister Joyce's cottage. All together we'd had a lovely trip; even the car ride there and back was passed pleasantly as we and our grandchildren listened to C.S. Lewis' *Narnia* stories on audio book.

I smiled as I remembered all the endless miles we once traveled with our own young children, me reading these same stories aloud to them to pass the time. Aslan's voice was deep and sonorous; it roared like a waterfall as we listened to this audio version. In fact, at the sound of that voice I had goose bumps as we drove along.

Now here we were, at the condo, remembering our trip and reflecting, waiting for the sunset color show to begin. Dave and Julie had just come to pick up their children, Caleb, Maddie, Alex, and Lilly, to take them home. It had been a glorious summer day with perfect waves for jumping, surfing, and floating. We were all sunbaked and tired, but happy.

That Sunday night we were to drive in to Grand Rapids for our small group meeting. "I'm too tired to go," Steve said.

I tried to talk him in to it. "I'll drive if you want," I said. He said he was going to stay home, but that I should go. I'm so grateful I decided to stay home. For supper, I made BLT's from the tomatoes just ripened on the vines from our patio pots.

Steve had tended those plants with loving care; part of his farmer self coming out. (In our Grand Rapids home on Breton Road, on a Saturday for fun Steve would work on our acreage property, trimming trees, completing little cement job repairs on the driveway, or water drainage projects. He could be out there all day. It was a good way for him to de-stress.)

My husband and I sat and ate by the window, then grabbed cups of coffee to go watch the sunset from the landing. Sitting and sipping our brew, we relaxed and watched the glory of God brushed across the expanse of sky as far as the eye could see.

Pink turned to amber to shades of violet and fuchsia. From the Master Artist's palette, He blended shades of blue—what a Creator we have! The sky sparkled with stars, and we made our way back up to our home away from home, never knowing we had just shared our last sunset together on this earth.

Chapter 18

Steve's Homegoing

Yet I am always with you, you hold me by my right hand. You guide me with your counsel, and afterward you will take me into glory (Psalm 73:23).

Surely He has carried our sorrows and our griefs (The Messiah by G.F. Handel).

The ending came on a simple ordinary day as endings often do. I was out of town, visiting my daughter and grandchildren on the East Coast.

"Jesus, help me. Jesus, help me! Jesus, help me …"

Dave and Jean, my friends and upstairs neighbors at the lake condo told me those three words were the only words I cried out, over and over, on that hardest of days. Once again, I was crying out to Jesus for help. I have never needed him so much.

The Wednesday before my world was turned upside down, I had traveled from Grand Rapids to Pennsylvania. Steve had dropped me off at the airport for my flight, on his way to a medical breakfast at the Spinnaker Hotel. He told me later that he had a "funny" feeling when he dropped me off. (I think this was a spiritual intuition given by the Holy Spirit and unrelated to his physical heart.)

Once I arrived at the airport, I discovered that my flight had been cancelled. No problem—I would just call Deb and let her know that I would be scheduling a later flight. But I had also lost my plane ticket, and this was before the days where you just show up and swipe your phone to get your boarding pass. To add insult to injury, the zipper in my suitcase broke as I was rummaging through it looking for my ticket.

Were these all signs that I shouldn't be going on this trip? I wondered. Later, Steve said I had been "discombobulated"—that's the word he used to my sister when she called the house that evening. Yes, I was a little bit panicked, out of sorts, and unnerved. Something was off. I just didn't know then what it was.

Steve answered his page right away at the medical breakfast. He said he'd come and pick me up to go home since the rescheduled flight was several hours later. His quick response to my page was unusual. Usually he didn't drop everything. I like to think that he didn't have to baby me. After all, I had traveled a lot and taken more plane trips than I can count. When Steve picked me up at the airport, I shared my apprehensions with him.

"Should I go at all?" I asked, as I wondered about the circumstances.

"Yes, of course," he replied in his unwavering way. "We prayed about this trip (as we did for all of our trips and plans), and Deborah has tickets for all the activities you will be doing together in New York City—the American Doll tea, etc." He was in no doubt: I should go as planned.

Looking back, that affirmation from Steve was a comfort to me as I thought about it later. By this time, we discovered someone had turned in my ticket at the airport. That person had found it at the other end of the building. Go figure.

We drove home, where I repacked the contents of my suitcase in Steve's suitcase. He insisted upon this because of the broken zipper. In retrospect this seems symbolic. Was he passing the ministry on to me? He fiddled with the zipper on my luggage and fixed it, but I still ended up taking his on the trip. Just before leaving for the airport again, I walked into our kitchen where Steve was getting a glass of water.

Suddenly I began crying from my very gut. I was sobbing from the center of my being, and I had no inkling why. I had traveled without Steve many times, and yet I was wailing as if I was going off to war and we would never see each other again. (In a way, I was headed into a war—the war of grief and loss.)

"I don't … know why … I'm crying," I managed to blubber out. Steve came over to me and put his arms around me. He prayed over me the armor of God, piece by piece.

"The helmet of salvation," my husband invoked. "The breastplate of righteousness. The sword of the spirit. The shield of faith. The belt of truth. And the shoes of the gospel of peace."

Then he kissed me goodbye, told me that he loved me and said something that I will never forget.

"You're going to be okay," he said. "You will be okay."

I believe Steve's words were a prophetic pronouncement for my future life, meant to encourage me many times in the years to come. And it was true—I was okay. By God's grace, I am okay, just as my husband predicted.

That was the last time I ever saw him. I boarded a flight for Philadelphia, forty-five minutes from Yardley, PA, where Deb and family lived, never knowing how my life would soon change. It was July 27, 2005.

That same night at Deb's house I called Steve and we reminisced about the good life that we had had together. He was a good husband and took great care of me. We took care of each other. I had been reading a book by Staci Eldridge on the plane, and she had written that every man wants to be a hero. (Thank you, Staci.)

"You're my hero, Steve," I said, concluding the call. Those were my last words to him. And he was … and is.

On the Thursday of that week, we took my granddaughter Campbell to the American Girl Doll Place in New York City to celebrate her seventh birthday. She had brought two of her cousins, Meagan and Kristen, from Kent's side of the family, and we had a wonderful day.

Deb had sewed matching outfits for the dolls and the girls, and of course they looked adorable standing on the train platform, waiting for our ride into the Big Apple. I was happy and proud as I heard the train whistle, delighted to be Grandma on such a day.

That night, as we traveled back to Pennsylvania by train, Steve called us and spoke to Deb. We were tired but happy after a long and sweet day, enjoying the little girls and their enchantment with the dolls. "I can just picture Mom and the fun she's had," he told Deb.

Friday evening, he left a message on Deb's answering machine, just checking in. He had just returned from the Ottawa County Fair and mentioned that he'd eaten a piece of rhubarb pie. "Mom's favorite, just for her," he said. Food—always a language of love in our family!

Steve was to speak to Deborah one more time. On Saturday, there was a wedding in which Campbell was the flower girl. Deborah and I had an emotional, hard discussion over something—can't remember what it was, and she wanted to call her dad and talk it over with him. She made the call between the wedding and the reception, around 11:45 a.m. in the late morning.

"A soft answer turns away wrath." Steve had quoted Scripture to her. He liked to see his role in the family as something like the Holy Spirit, reconciling and bringing peace to us all. Those were his last words to his daughter.

Now we know that he died while Deborah was talking to him. "I heard some noise but just thought it was static on the call. So I hung up and dialed again but it was busy," she said. We had no way of knowing he would die at around noon, soon after the call.

On Saturday night I tried calling him, but the line was busy. I wasn't concerned because at the time we had dial-up internet and he was also making travel plans for both of us to go to India for a time of teaching and ministry. Additionally, I knew that he had been invited to a neighbor's open house party.

About twenty-four hours after Deborah had talked to her dad on Saturday noon, I said to Deb, "Let's just check in with Dad before we leave for church." Now it's Sunday morning.

When I couldn't reach Steve by phone, I rang his beeper (as a doctor, Steve was on call 24/7 so he always carried a beeper with him and he always answered it.) After two tries, when my husband didn't answer his beeper, I called David and Jean, our upstairs neighbors at our lake condo.

"Could you please go down to our condo and tell Steve to put the phone back on the hook?" I asked them. "And tell him to call me."

We had trouble with cell phones at the lake, and there were multiple buttons on our landlines. Between the lake house and the Grand

Rapids house, we'd sometimes get confused and press the wrong button inadvertently. I assumed that Steve had done that and had left the phone off the hook.

David and Jean went downstairs, as I had asked. They knocked and rang the bell, but no one came to the door. Fortunately, the door was unlocked, and they went inside our condo, calling for Steve. When they wandered into our bedroom, they found him lying stretched out on our bed. He was dead.

They told me later that even through their shock they observed that Steve was peaceful, lazily stretched out on the bed, watching the Weather Channel. Beside him on the bed lay a half-eaten grilled cheese sandwich on a paper plate and a half-consumed Diet Coke. The phone lay on his chest, off the hook. My husband Steve had already passed from this world to the next. He was in Heaven.

What a life-changing assignment I had asked of my neighbors! They are believers, and they decided to rally support and intervention for me before they gave me the news. David and Jean called another Christian couple close by, and they gathered together to pray for me and my children, knowing their phone call would bear the hardest news we had ever faced.

Meantime, Deborah and I were waiting for that phone call from Steve. It seemed like a long time but it probably wasn't more than 20 minutes. When the phone did ring, my daughter ran to the phone. I saw the absolute terror and panic on her face.

I grabbed the phone from her and heard the news that would tear me in two. "*Jesus, help me. Jesus, help me! Jesus…*" I knew I could not survive the experience of losing Steve without my Lord. I couldn't make it for a single moment without God's strength and love.

It was July 31, 2005, the day after Steve died. It was the first day of the rest of my life without him.

***

Much of what followed that phone call was a blur. Kent made plans for Deb and I to fly home to Grand Rapids on the next available flight; he and the children would drive separately.

At the airport gate, waiting for the flight, Deborah noticed a Hispanic woman coughing and choking, fighting for breath and holding her stomach in pain. The woman had a baby in arms, a toddler, and a school-aged child. Deborah ran over with a bottle of water to see if she could help. Deb spoke Spanish, so she was able to communicate with them.

She could tell this was a serious situation and called for me to come over and assist. I quickly went to the desk and they announced a medical emergency. Reaching out to help others in need, Deb and I were transported away from our emotional space for a little while.

We stayed with the woman and her children for about twenty minutes while they waited for the first responders. Deborah spoke with her in Spanish as I prayed over her. Soon the lady was loaded onto a stretcher and carried away and we both returned to our seats.

"See," I heard a voice inside say, "I'm not finished with you yet." Those words from my Father were and are a great comfort to me to this day.

Arriving in Grand Rapids, we were met by David and Julie and their children—who had beat a hasty retreat from vacationing on Saginaw Bay after I called them—and a crowd of loving people. Our church small group and other close friends were there as well to surround us in their loving arms. There was solace in the arms of those who cared for us.

David, Deborah, and I drove immediately to the funeral home. Before I had left Pennsylvania, I had given instructions over the phone. "Don't do anything to him," I requested. I also directed them to keep Steve's body wrapped in the quilt from our bed where they found him.

In my shock, I guess I still wanted to take care of him and make sure he was comfortable. I always loved nurturing and caring for my husband. A quilt seemed friendlier than a crinkly plastic, zippered body bag. It had been a shocking sight for my lake neighbors to see my strong husband, carried out to a funeral hearse on a sunny Sunday morning enfolded in bedding.

At the funeral home, I approached Steve's body alone. "I have to hear from you, Lord, or I can't make it," I begged God in prayer. "Speak to me." In the past, I had taught many retreats on listening to God, using the passage in John 10:27, "My sheep hear my voice." If I ever desperately need to hear his voice it was now.

Two weeks before, returning from the family reunion in Canada, as I've already mentioned, we had listened to "*The Lion, the Witch and the Wardrobe*" by C.S. Lewis on audio. When I heard Aslan's sonorous voice, I had shivers. *Jesus is the Lion of Judah*! I marveled.

Now, standing by my husband's body, I again heard Aslan's voice. Six statements:

"I'm in control.

You're not.

I know the future.

You don't.

This was a better way.

I saved you from a disaster."

Instinctively I knew. God was telling me that had I been with Steve when he died, it would have been far worse. I would not have accepted the fact of his death and would have gone to any length at all to somehow make it not true.

Steve's cardiac doctor assured me and my children that Steve's death had been instantaneous and peaceful. If I had been there, even in the next room or right beside him, there would have been nothing I could have done to help him. But knowing myself, I would have gutted myself trying.

"This was a better way ... I saved you from a disaster."

I thought so much about those words, turning them over in my head. What did it mean?

Steve could have fallen off his bike while we were taking a bike ride together. He could have been behind the wheel and hurt or killed us both and others. He could have died a few days earlier when we were all jumping gleefully in the Lake Michigan waves with our grandchildren. How traumatic that would have been for them and for all of us, perhaps ruining the lake for us all.

I came to thank God for sparing us from whatever disaster He had in mind when He spoke to me at the funeral home. God's way of Steve's death was the better, more peaceful way. The end of Steve's life could hardly have been more calm and serene. One moment he was talking to his daughter on the phone, lounging on his bed, watching the Weather Channel, and the next he was flown to his heavenly home.

Yet, I know given the chance to do it all over again, I never would have left Steve's side. God, in his perfect wisdom and kindness, removed me from that harrowing situation.

Aslan's words—God's words—brought me supernatural comfort and strength, then and now. Thus fortified, I could negotiate the next days of shock and grief, and all the planning that needed to be done.

***

Later, the Lord graciously gave me a vision of exactly what had happened during Steve's homegoing. I saw two angels enter our bedroom through the sliding door at the condo. One went to either side of Steve's body and together they carefully lifted him up.

"One, two, three ... okay," one of them said as they lifted Steve. Then they flew away, carrying Steve's spirit to his Maker. I recognized the angels in my vision. I had seen them before.

Ten years before, Steve had to undergo open-heart surgery. That day, ten years before Steve's death, I had just returned from a pilgrimage to Toronto to attend a Billy Graham Crusade and to mark with thanksgiving the forty-year anniversary of when I committed my life to Jesus.

While I was gone, Steve experienced chest pains and David insisted that he go to urgent care. From there, they rushed him to a hospital by ambulance. He was told by his cardiologist that he needed bypass surgery as soon as possible. Of course, I flew home as fast as I could to be by Steve's side at the hospital. As he was lying semiconscious in the pre-surgical room, hooked up to a heart pump and awaiting surgery, I had a question for the Lord.

Several pastors and David and I had already anointed Steve with oil. Steve would say later that I called every pastor in town! They had come and gone now. The room was silent except for the beeping of the heart pump to which Steve was attached.

"Lord, what should I do now?" again I inquired. I looked down at my open purse and saw the crisp, white song sheet from the Billy Graham Crusade folded inside. I spotted the lyrics of a favorite song.

"This is my story, this is my song, praising my Savior, all the day long." I took it as a direct communication.

"Lord, you want me to praise you now?" Well, who was I to argue with God?

I began to praise God and thank him that He was in control. Suddenly, I felt something akin to liquid joy falling from heaven and permeating every cell of my body. My soul was saturated with molten joy—that's the only way I can describe it. As I sang in obedience, I stopped suddenly when I got to a certain verse from the song:

"Angels descending, look from above, visions of mercy, fountains of love."

"Lord, could you please send some angels?" It didn't hurt to ask, and in this case, I received a prompt answer.

Two angels stood before me, one at the head of Steve's bed and the other one at the foot.

Wow! This is amazing. I think I'll ask for more angels, I thought.

"Lord, will you please send an angel to attend to the cardiac surgeon, and one for the anesthesiologist, and one for the doctor managing the heart pump?"

Silence. And then, a vision within a vision: I could picture our Father with a smile on his face.

"Only five angels? You're on a roll. Why don't I send an even half dozen, and the sixth one can be the circulating nurse/angel?" I heard God's words in my spirit, and peace washed over me. My Father's attending angels would be on the job. There was no need to worry.

Yes, I recognized those angels that were there in my vision at Steve's death. Did Steve have a feeling of familiarity when those same two messengers transported him to Heaven? I won't know until I join him there someday.

***

I do look forward to the hope of heaven someday. I hope it will be a long time from now because I still have a lot of living to do. I was reminded yesterday by our longtime friends that I had said exactly that in my eulogy at Steve's funeral service.

"I still have a lot of living to do." I did. And I do!

At the time of this writing, it's been almost fifteen years since that day when my life was unalterably changed. God has been faithful, and Jesus has helped me more times than I can possibly count. I am happy and content and relish a lovely, full life in this "new normal" since Steve died. Yes, I still miss the love of my life and always will. But by God's grace, I am making it and making it well.

Dear reader, if you put your faith in Jesus, you will find a God who cares for you. He is with us all through life and death. I encourage you to place all the details of your life in his safekeeping. I'm not just talking about the big decisions and burdens, but every small, seemingly mundane thing.

He has cared for me in such a personal, meticulous way, and He will do the same for you. If you cry out to God, as I have done so many times and as I did when I received the news of Steve's death, He will respond to you lovingly and with all the concern in his Father's heart. And He will point you to Heaven, your forever home.

Life with Jesus is full of reminders that the road we're traveling together is ultimately a road to heaven. When you consider this magnificent last stop on the journey, the road ahead becomes much less important.

One other incident: Later that summer of 2005, after Steve's death, I was floating in Lake Michigan, peering at the gorgeous sky, and pondering our beautiful, sad goodbye on that Wednesday, July 27th. As I drifted on the water, I suddenly realized that that day would have been my mother's 100th birthday, had she lived.

Did my dear mother, as a loving intercessor among the "cloud of witnesses," have something to do with our goodbye and Steve's comfort-giving assertion that I would be okay? I took it as a ray of light from Paradise, a hint of my future with loved ones.

Friends of mine gave me a copy of the devotional "Jesus Calling," by Sarah Young. Just today, on July 27th, the anniversary of my last goodbye to Steve, I read the following:

"I am training you to hold in your heart a dual focus: My continual presence and the hope of heaven."

You and I may still have some living to do. Possibly a whole lot of it! May we do so holding God's constant company and the dream of eternity in dual focus—close to our hearts.

Chapter 19

A New Life Beckoning

Do not be afraid, you will not suffer shame. Do not fear disgrace, you will not be humiliated. You will forget the shame of your youth and remember no more the reproach of your widowhood. For Your Maker is your husband, the Lord Almighty is His name, the Holy One of Israel is your Redeemer, he is called the God of all the earth (Isaiah 54:4).

I had no idea how to move forward. I knew I could only do it with God's help. There were so many decisions to make. *Jesus, help me!*

After the burial we had to find a tombstone. Where does one go to find that? I was still grieving and emotionally depleted. My friend, Kris, found some tombstone stores and off we went to look at memorial stones.

The following Scripture has always meant a lot to me. I've sung it over and over again in my musical theatre rendition of "The Ballad of Mary and Martha" when Martha questions Jesus about his delay in coming to raise her brother Lazarus from the dead. Jesus answers Martha by replying:

I am the resurrection and the life. The one who believes in me will live, even though they die; and whoever lives by believing in me will never die. Do you believe this? (John 11:25, 26).

This verse appears on Steve's tombstone and is such a comfort to me. I wanted this verse to be etched in stone so that the generations after me would be challenged by Jesus' question to Martha: "Do you believe this?" May you be challenged and comforted by the Holy Spirit of God.

After Steve's death, I had to mourn, and I mourned deeply. Lots of tears for quite a while.

I remember one Sunday afternoon, listening to my praise music and "soaking" in God's Presence. Music helped me so incredibly. I was recalling a few weeks before Steve died. We had won the prize (a dollar bill) for the longest married couple on the dance floor.

Now I was imagining myself in Steve's arms as we danced to Elvis's song, *Love me tender, love me true.* I was enjoying the memory, when suddenly in a vision I saw Jesus approaching us. He said, "May I have this dance?"

Steve answered assuredly, "Oh yes, Lord, take her." I eagerly went into Jesus' arms and began to dance, floating effortlessly around the dance floor following his lead, with almost no effort on my part.

I was so joyful, exuberant, satisfied. Then I looked around for Steve, and … he was gone. He had handed me over to Jesus, the lover of my soul. Yes, deep grief, and we need to grieve, but also joy in knowing that we are not alone.

Adjustments

I had a huge adjustment to make—life without my husband. As I look back over these fifteen years of the "New Normal," I am filled with gratefulness, contentment, and joy, most of the time but certainly not always fully.

Yes, the shock and the grief of Steve's death was deep. At times the agony and tears were so deep, I couldn't catch my breath. I wondered if I could keep living in so much pain.

Countless times over these years, I have prayed my simple prayer that began as a young child: "*Jesus, help me.*" And He has, in big and small ways. It says in Isaiah 54:5 that the Lord is a husband to us, and God has been that for me. A friend gave me this Scripture verse after Steve died:

Fear not, you will forget the shame and reproach and confusion of your widowhood. For your Maker is your husband, the Lord of hosts is his name, your Redeemer, the God of the whole earth. (Isaiah 54:5)

There were so many things to learn—finances, the car, the yard—all the tasks Steve traditionally took care of. We seemed to divide our tasks that way. I especially missed Steve in times of crises.

In fact, right now as I edit this manuscript we are in a time of a pandemic crisis, a worldwide war with the Corona Covid 19 virus, the invisible enemy! We're told to stay indoors to protect ourselves. Everything is closed down. So, I am in a present time of crisis and find that I'm missing Steve more, being isolated and alone.

One time in the past in our large family home the hot water tank blew up and flooded the basement; another time the outside irrigation system malfunctioned and flooded the cracks in the cement walls. My car started on fire on the way to Toronto. My house was broken into while I was on a trip. The garage doors refused to open when I was on my way to a crucial appointment.

And, oh yes, my living room ceiling collapsed, threatening to take out my grand piano, and maybe my head on the one-year anniversary of Steve's death. You couldn't even make up these things if you tried!

Crash of the Living Room Ceiling

It was the one-year anniversary of Steve's death, a beautiful, sunny, but very hot day. The sunshine was beaming into my living room through the front windows as I relaxed and journaled my prayers to the Lord.

"Lord, it's been a year now; what do you want me to do with this house?"

He and I had been talking about it for a while. My grandchildren loved this old family home situated on a ravine and several acres of wooded property where they could hike, sled, and sometimes even skate on the small frozen creek. They sure didn't want Gramma to sell her house!

Realistically, the property was too big for just one person. The upkeep and maintenance were no small thing. And the house needed to be updated. Lounging in my peach colored armchair, I looked forward to Deborah and her children arriving soon from Pennsylvania so that we could be together for this one year anniversary.

I wanted it to be a special day of remembrance and had planned a slide show for the grandchildren of their parents when they were babies, special food, and a special dinner out at our favorite family Chinese restaurant. I had copies made of Steve's photo to place in sweet little silver frames for each of the grandchildren.

"Ring, ring, ring!" I was lifted out of my reverie and clumsily rose from my armchair. I was still recovering from a total knee replacement surgery and wasn't very spry yet. To be truthful, spryness is not one of my great attributes anyway. I answered the phone in the kitchen. It was my friend Cindy calling to tell me that she could make the prints of Steve's photo on her computer.

As I hung up the phone, I heard a thundering crash coming from the living room. I hustled as quickly as my recovering knee would allow to see what had happened. Out of my mouth and gut came a very loud authoritative declarative: "*No!*"

The living room ceiling was falling in. The chair I had been sitting in minutes before was squashed. The ceiling boards had crashed and splintered the lamps and were precariously dangling over the open lid of my grand piano. But the wreckage stopped when my "*No!*" burst through the atmosphere.

My piano was intact, my treasured oil painting over the mantle was in one piece, and thankfully, my head was still attached. Thank you, Lord Jesus.

I called Dave and he and the family came right over. Ron and Mary, my trusted neighbors, came over. We sawed the pieces of the fallen ceiling wallboard and put them on the front lawn. It looked like a war zone when Deborah and her family arrived. (Later, we found out that the ceiling had caved in because it was glued together, not joined with a hammer and nails. The excessive heat had caused not just my roof to collapse but others on the same road.)

Alex, who was four years old at the time, and very sensitive to me and my feelings, spoke up. "What are you going to do, Gramma?"

"Maybe this is a sign that God wants me to sell the house." Alex liked to play in the ravine and did not want me to sell. I could see the wheels turning in his little head, and after a few moments he gathered up his sweet, small chest, raising his head commandingly.

"I'm God," he boomed, as much as a little guy like that could boom. "Don't sell the house."

As it turned out, I finally did sell the house eight years later. Steve and I had put the house on the market a couple of times before he died, and I had listed the house several times since his death, but there were no takers. This house with its five bedrooms, a large downstairs family room, and a two-room office over the garage was kind of an anomaly. Much of the house was outdated and needed renovation.

When God's timing was right, everything happened quickly. I had come home one night from the lake condo and the thought came to me clearly: *I'm ready to sell this house, as is. I don't want to do the work of updating or spend the money to do it. I'd rather travel!*

I called my realtor, Ryan, who had listed my home the year before. "Do you have anyone interested in buying my house?"

One year before, a couple had seen the house and were interested but had to sell their house first. The timing was impeccable as God's timing always is. It turned out that the couple was still interested, and in fact Ryan was going to list their home that very night. A Christian family moved into my home, for which I had wanted and prayed.

The next morning, I called Holland Home to see if there were any homes available and there was one. They showed me a nice condo, I bought it, and here I am.

"For your Maker is your husband ..." I am still pondering and praising God for the reality of that verse. I have turned to the Lord in countless situations and asked him, "Lord, what shall I do?" He answers as my husband would.

"Call this person," the thought comes. "Call that one." I am not alone—far from it. God provided a lovely group of friends, neighbors and family who came over to help or give me advice. With my Maker as my husband, it has all worked out according to his master plan.

The Disaster Cruise

Sometimes, though, it's hard to trust the unseen and believe that all things do work together for good. Life has a way of knocking you down with its obstacles and challenges. The family cruise stands out as one of those difficult moments.

I planned a trip for myself and my two children and their families to go on a Disney cruise on the second New Years after Steve's death. I wanted to make it a healing time of togetherness and memories. My investment toward that end was significant, paying for all the flights and cruise fare for twelve people.

The night before we were to board the cruise ship, four of the five Kings who stayed in my hotel room were violently ill. We thought it might have been food poisoning. Unfortunately, it's standard procedure in cruising that you will be asked upon check in if anyone in your party has been sick.

When I learned this, I was severely conflicted. What should I do? Should I lie? Ugh. I thought about all the money I had spent. I asked my kids what to do. "You are the matriarch," said Dave. "Do what you think." Great! Apparently, I can't pawn this decision on anyone but myself.

I told the truth as best I could, hoping they would have mercy. "Even though everyone is presently okay, last night two of the kids were sick and throwing up," I explained. "But we do think it was food poisoning and not the flu."

After much deliberation with the ship's medical people, the King family was denied boarding. All the King kids and their cousins were crying in the terminal. They had to get their bags off the ship and I had to decide what to do. It all seemed so unfair.

One of my biggest regrets is I didn't cancel the whole trip for all of us so that we could do it later. At the time, things were so chaotic, and the pressure was on to make a snap decision. So, we decided I would join the Allens on the cruise and the Kings would return home to Michigan.

It seemed like a disaster and my mood had soured. I boarded with the Allen family and basically cried, obsessed, and fussed my way through the cruise. I was utterly heart broken. The King family did get a voucher to go on a later cruise, but we were not together.

My big plan to have a healing family reunion blew up in my face. Aside from Steve's death, this disaster was the worst thing that ever happened to me. The defeated feeling continued when I returned home and I sunk into a depression about the whole fiasco.

In retrospect, it was probably too soon for me after Steve's death to plan such a major vacation. Interestingly, in recent conversation, the Allens talked about what a good time they had. (*Ha! Oh, well. At least someone had fun on that cruise.*)

Fun and Ministry Opportunities

In my New Normal without Steve, I've had lots of opportunities to travel for conferences, board meetings, teaching and ministry opportunities—some work related but some just for fun. I took several cruises with friends and my sisters to the French Riviera, the Caribbean, the Baltic Sea, Alaska, the Panama Canal, The United Kingdom, Ireland, and Western Canada.

In 2013, I was invited by Freedom in Christ to teach sessions in Trinidad on depression, anxiety, fear, substance abuse, and emotions. Most of the seminars were co-sponsored by the Catholic Church.

As we praised God together, holding hands in a circle, honoring the Lord Jesus, and asking for the anointing of the Holy Spirit, I had a *Deja vu* moment. I remembered fellowshipping with the Catholic sisters in the small villages of North West Territories forty-five years before. I had come full circle again and was grateful.

Prior to Steve's death, I had been invited to speak in several venues at Christ for the Nations, our beloved *alma mater* Bible Institute in Dallas, Texas. I have returned many times to speak and teach. *God is still using me*, I thought.

I am so thankful. I love teaching and felt very fulfilled, especially the relishing time with the Lindsay family. I did consider Freda's offer of moving to Dallas and teaching at CFNI, but it didn't seem to be in God's plan for me.

Africa

When Steve was still alive, he and I traveled together to Africa for the first time, visiting Liberia in 2003 over Christmas time. We accompanied our new friend, Christine Tolbert Norman, the daughter of the former President of Liberia, William Tolbert, who had been assassinated in a bloody coup in 1980.

Earlier, we had met Christine at a Freedom in Christ conference where Steve and I had been doing a seminar on depression together. Steve talked about medical interventions as a psychiatrist and I taught on the other aspects of the soul (will, mind, emotions) and the spirit. After the lecture, Christine approached us. "I want you to come to Africa with me and teach the Freedom in Christ material," she said.

We suggested that we go out for lunch and talk more. Christine explained that she had a cousin named Georgia who had been chained to a bed post because she was crazy and out of control. Georgia lived in a small village some distance from the capital city of Monrovia. Christine wondered for the first time after hearing our presentation, if maybe medication could help this dear soul.

Christine returned to Liberia and got in touch with the one psychiatrist in all the country, Dr. Grant. Accompanied by a nurse, he visited Georgia in her village, gave her a shot, and took her to his small psychiatric hospital for treatment. Her psychosis was healed by the medication, and Georgia returned to her village in her right mind.

A *miracle* of medication, for sure, but God is the Healer who invented the medication and created a body to receive the medication and be healed. Two months later, Christine called us from Liberia with the good news about Georgia.

I had just finished writing a book with Dr. Neil Anderson and Dr. Fernando Garson entitled "*Released from Bondage.*" Georgia's story was a pithy example of our book title! Elated by this miracle, a seed planted in my heart: I wanted to go to Africa and meet these people myself. Steve had been asking me what I wanted to do for my 60th birthday coming up. Did I want to go on a cruise or another kind of trip?

"Africa," I said. "I want to go to Africa." Steve was not enthused and tried to talk me out of it. In the meantime, Christine had invited us to meet her in Liberia to accompany her back to her hometown for her first Christmas there since she had fled the country. After her father and brother were murdered, she had been exiled to Coite d'Ivoire (The Ivory Coast).

I prayed that if God wanted us to go on this trip He would have to change Steve's mind. Instead of exerting all kinds of energy trying to persuade Steve to go, like I had done too many times in the past, I left it with God. I had been learning to do that little by little.

Realizing that we are not the Holy Spirit in relationships is a good thing. I was grateful then, when Steve went to a prayer meeting at church and came home afterwards and announced that he was now willing to go. Yippee! God had done his work.

We spent that Christmas with Christine and the team, walking through the gun-toting barricades of the United Nations Army and visiting orphanages. We taught a seminar on Freedom in Christ and hung our Christmas stockings on a palm tree. Yes, we visited Georgia in her village, too. What an exhilarating memory for me, praising God with Georgia in the deep dark under the African stars, singing "How Great Thou Art."

The psychiatric hospital had no electricity as their generator had been stolen. There was no light, no refrigeration for medication, and no mattresses on the beds because of thievery. People were desperate due to ongoing wars and factions.

Steve and I decided that for our Christmas gift to each other, we would buy a generator and mattresses for the hospital. Wonderfully, the lights came on Christmas Eve. What a loving metaphor of our Savior, who had been born to bring light and life to the world!

Dr. Stephen King Memorial Library

For Steve's funeral, I requested that donations be made in lieu of flowers to Freedom in Christ International. After these donations were disbursed, I asked Christine about the greatest need in Liberia.

She suggested a library in Bentol, her birth town, where there were hardly any books, even in the school. It also was the town where Georgia lived. The *Dr. Stephen King Memorial Library* was born. Since then it has been expanded to twice its size and has become a valuable resource for the community and the school.

In 2008, after Steve was gone and in my new normal, I traveled to Africa by myself to teach more of the Freedom in Christ material to pastors and government workers and to visit the library in Bentol. We had a marvelously fun celebration party with the children and teachers of the village.

From Liberia, I flew to South Africa where I participated in another Freedom in Christ teaching with Dr. Neil Anderson and my South African friend and psychiatrist, Dr. Carina le Roux. Carina took vacation days so that we could travel down the East Coast of Africa to Cape Town at the southern tip.

On the way, we went on an exquisite Safari, enjoying more of God's creation, including elephants, lions, zebras, giraffes and hippos! I was surprised and delighted to see penguins in their natural habitat in a preserve in Cape Town.

Shortly after meeting Christine, I became a member of her REAP (Restoration and Education of Advancement Programs) board for the impoverished youth of Liberia. Christine had held the position of Deputy Minister of Education at the time of her father's death, and as an educator she had started schools in Monrovia and the Ivory Coast.

Christine spent a season as the mayor of Bentol, the same city where the library is located, and I am a board member to this day. I enjoy regular visits from Christine when she is stateside. She calls me her "twin sister" since we're the same age.

One time at a talent night during a Freedom in Christ Conference we did a two-step dance across the platform in matching dresses, with Christine wearing a long blonde wig, as we sang, "The twins go marching two by two, hoorah, hoorah." Oh well, sometimes it's fun to be crazy.

***

Loss of my Siblings

When Steve died, I cherished my relationships with my siblings even more, especially with my sisters, Joyce and Barb. They were my closest friends growing up and also as adults. We often remarked how blessed we were to be best friends and sisters.

I have saved so many of the loving sister cards that they gave me. We talked often, sometimes daily, keeping in close contact even though they lived in Canada and I lived in Michigan. We always knew what the other was up to. Writing this book has stirred so many memories of my dear sisters and what they meant to me.

I think fondly of the trip we took to Ireland, our ancestral home, in the fall of 2010. Joyce and Barb and I had a fascinating trip tracing our Irish roots. We went by bus and car, visiting old churches and graveyards to follow up on the information which we had received from an Irish genealogist beforehand.

Experiencing together this beautiful country with its lush green fields dotted with mama sheep and her babies was exquisite. My sisters and I had so much fun, laughing and talking and sharing our excitement. Maybe we had too much fun—the tour director called us

"The Terrible Three." Certainly, we put the terror into "Terrible Three" as we navigated Ireland's narrow, hedge-lined roads.

I was the designated driver by default and we were all nervous—a first for me driving on the opposite side of the road from what I was used to. Barb was sitting in the front seat with me and thought she was having a panic attack. So we stopped.

Joyce, seated in the back seat, kept feeding me chocolate. The angels were busy that day! But we made it out alive and with no damage to the car. That was my spoken goal as we began our road trip.

Our mother had never been back to Ireland and we all wanted to live that experience for her. I have a large notebook crammed with the information from our discoveries, and most of all I have a deeply meaningful memory. Unbeknown to me, our time as three sisters was waning. Soon we would be two.

Joyce

In September of 2011, Joyce was driving to a dinner party when she suffered a stroke. She had slowed down, the flowers and the chocolates on the front seat hurtling forward as she put her foot on the brake. She was uninjured but when the police arrived she was incoherent and taken immediately to the hospital.

We thought we were going to lose her that day, but she lingered in the ICU for several days in an unconscious state. Many prayers went forward on her behalf. In fact, it was during that time that I was in Dallas speaking at the Healing Seminar. Bill Johnston and Heidi Baker prayed for Joyce and me at that time.

It was a difficult time, especially since Joyce's daughter, Jill, who was undergoing chemotherapy for breast cancer, was in a weakened state. Joyce quite miraculously recovered in the hospital and was moved to an intermediate care room as she regained some of her speech and cognition. We all were able to express our love, which was a blessing, as was the fact that I could visit her every few weeks.

All of us were hoping for continuing recovery when she suffered another debilitating brain bleed and went into another coma. She died in late December of that year, an incredible loss to her family and for my sister Barb and me.

Barbara-Jo

Barb and I had another two years together before she, too, left this earth for Heaven. In late fall, 2012, Barb laid in the hospital bed in Newmarket, Ontario, seriously ill with stage 4 metastatic bone cancer. We were later told that the origin of the bone cancer was from the breast.

She had been admitted to the hospital in September. I was scheduled to travel to Trinidad for ministry. I reluctantly left the country, worried about my little sister. I left phone numbers with her family and went ahead.

Upon returning to Michigan, I was anxious to get to Newmarket, where Barb was languishing and in severe pain. She was unable to move herself out of the bed. I was overcome with grief when I saw how she was suffering.

"I don't know how to pray for you, Barb," I said. Should I pray for her death since she is in so much pain or should I pray for her healing? It became another lesson in healing prayer.

Together we stopped and asked the Lord, "How should we pray?" The Lord gave me another prayer picture, but in this case, I was quite disconcerted with it. It was Barb, alive in her swimming pool.

Lord, I'm wondering if you've got this one wrong, I prayed. Barb is dying and it's December with three feet of snow on the ground and sub-zero temperatures. How presumptuous of me that I should question my God, the Lord and Creator of the Universe! But actually I was really wondering if that thought was just from me, as a hopeful wish.

When I continued in my silence and checked my heart, I knew this picture was from him, even with my lack of faith. So we prayed for Barb to recover and someday swim in her swimming pool. I know I had no faith as I prayed. Perhaps Barb did.

That Christmas, Barb checked herself out of the hospital to be home in hospice care. Astonishingly, with excellent daily nursing support from her nurse, Carol, my sister lived until the following December. During that time, we were able to go out to dinner, concerts, and movies. On her 65th birthday, we hosted a family reunion birthday party that Barby-Jo called "65 and Still Alive."

I totally forgot about the swimming pool prayer until the following June. My sweet sister texted me a photo of her swimming in her pool.

"Do you remember the prayer?" she texted. What a great reminder of the God who speaks to his children in many ways.

Towards the end of her life, Barb decided to go to a hospice center in Barry, Ontario, near her children's home. She didn't want her precious grandchildren to see her in such bad shape. I was honored to be with her, along with her adult children and spouses, when she took her last breath. It was another great loss for me in my "new normal," now a "new, new normal." I miss my two sisters intensely, and long to be with them again someday.

My brother Bruce had died in 2002 of an aneurism. The last time I spoke to him was on New Year's Eve, 2001. Steve had planned a surprise birthday party for me for my New Year's Day birthday. He secretly invited my sisters to fly from Ontario to surprise me.

Bruce was excited about his sisters being all together and forgot it was a surprise. "Have Barb and Joyce arrived there yet?" he asked me on the phone before their "surprise" arrival. Oh well, it was still great fun.

In 2015, my big brother Jim was the last of my siblings to die, also from an aneurism. All my siblings' spouses are also gone, except for my former sister-in-law, Mary Briggs, a beautiful, loving treasure for us all. I am left as the matriarch of a large family—twenty-eight nieces and nephews on my side of the family alone. I am blessed to have them in my life and enjoy sporadic connections and visits with them.

Surgeries

Looking back through these fifteen years since Steve died, I am especially grateful for God's provision for all my medical needs. Prior to losing Steve, I had never had a single surgery, so I was ill prepared for the onslaught to come.

There were two total knee replacements, double pulmonary embolisms twice, surgery for a compound fracture in my ankle (resulting in nine screws and a plate), and a broken rib from a fall.

I underwent the first knee replacement during the grief-stricken year after Steve's death. I went to every healing service I could find to pray for healing. How could I go through this without my doctor husband, with whom I had felt so secure and safe?

Please Lord, heal me. I can't go through this surgery without Steve, I prayed. But the pain kept getting worse until one day my friend Dean from Set Free Ministries called and asked how I was doing. I burst into tears and he offered to have me come for some prayer at his ministry.

"I've tried to have enough faith to be healed," I cried. "Why hasn't it happened"?

"Well," Dean said, "I think that you probably need more faith to go and get the surgery." The light bulb went off and I saw my error. I underwent the surgery and it was successful. When the doctor came out after the surgery to talk to my family, my son and daughter stood up along with eight members of my small group.

Those closest to me knew how scared I was. I was not alone. *Thank you, Lord. My knees, my ankle, my rib, and my lungs have been healed by your power and the expert medical intervention I have received. Thank you for being a husband to me all these years.*

A year later I had another knee replacement surgery and that also went well.

I'm able to travel, for which I'm thankful, although I must admit I had my doubts recently when I experienced the second bilateral pulmonary embolisms (clots in both of my lungs). I was thinking about my own mortality after my traumatic medical crisis and hospitalization, when I heard the lyrics of a praise song and it spoke to my heart. "I will run the race, til I see his face." And that's what I plan to do by God's grace.

Musing

For I know the plans I have for you, declares the Lord, plans to prosper you and not to harm you, plans to give you a hope and a future. (Jeremiah 29:11)

Conclusion

Yet I am always with you, you hold me by my right hand, You guide me with your counsel and *afterward* you will take me into glory (Psalm 73:24). [Italics mine]

After Steve's death, God told me I still had a lot of living to do, and He was right. But I must confess, I wondered in those early days of shock and grief if I wanted to live. How could I go on without my best friend and the love of my life?

Yet in his gracious way, God over time straightened me out about those thoughts—thoughts which are pretty normal after such a shocking death. Again He brought me to Scripture to light my way forward.

Psalm 73 shouted the answer to my soul:

When my heart was grieved and my spirit embittered,
I was senseless and ignorant; I was a brute beast before you.
Yet I am always with you; you hold me by my right hand.
You guide me with your counsel and *afterward* you will take me into glory.
Whom have I in heaven but you? And earth has nothing I desire besides you.
My flesh and my heart may fail, but God is the strength of my heart and my portion forever.
But as for me, it is good to be near God. I have made the Sovereign Lord my refuge. *I will tell of all your deeds*." (Psalm 73:21-26,28) [Italics mine]

God spoke to me very clearly about the word "*afterward*."

(*Afterward*: Later; subsequently. Then, next, after that.)

My Father still had work for me to do on earth before He would bring me to Heaven. It will only be *afterward*, after my death that

189

He will take me into his glory. To me it's not surprising God spoke to me through Scripture. I love the Bible, and He speaks to me so often as I am reading or meditating or singing it.

As you read about this journey of my life, my hopes for you are threefold:

- You will continue to follow Jesus as your Savior and to "be being" filled [continue to be filled] with the Holy Spirit, the Spirit of Truth and our Comforter.
- You will embrace Scripture as your touchstone and plant its precepts in your heart and brain.
- You will become as free as you were created to be, from the foundation of time.

Freedom in Christ Ministries

My involvement with Freedom in Christ Ministries has been transformational in my life. As mentioned before, our involvement with Freedom in Christ started in 1995. Steve served as a board member for FICM USA for several years, and then I replaced him on the board when he died.

Recently, I was elected for a second term to the Freedom in Christ International Board, representing North America and the Caribbean. In that role, I traveled to Mexico City in October 2018 to speak for the 10th anniversary of Mexico's Freedom in Christ Ministry.

The *Steps to Freedom*, the centerpiece of FICM's Discipleship Counseling Ministry, have been hugely influential in my spiritual development. The *Steps* have solidified my identity in Christ as a child of God. They continue to help me resolve spiritual conflicts and war against the powers of darkness, identifying Satan's lies and then replacing those lies with the truths of God's Word. They remind me to forgive consistently.

I strongly encourage you, my dear family and friends, to avail yourself of this spiritual tool. It will change your life as you allow the Holy Spirit to transform you. For those of us who have codependent tendencies, the truth that we can be who God wants us to be—not who anyone else thinks we should be or even who we think we should be—is liberating.

Philippians 4:13 says, "I can do all things through Christ who strengthens me." For people pleasers and/or perfectionists and for all who struggle, this truth sets us free. I *can* be who God wants me to be, and He is the One who strengthens me and helps me to do just that.

I urge you to get a copy of Dr. Neil Anderson's *Steps to Freedom*, a comprehensive spiritual inventory, and go through the *Steps* yourself. I take myself through the *Steps* regularly. In fact, as board members we are required to have an encourager lead us through these *Steps* every two years.

The Gospel

On a recent Tuesday morning FICM U.S. board prayer call, we heard the Word from John 14. I had memorized Jesus' words as a young adult and those words again penetrated my soul:

> "Do not let your hearts be troubled. You believe in God; believe in Me as well. In My Father's house are many rooms. If it were not so, would I have told you that I am going there to prepare a place for you? And if I go and prepare a place for you, I will come back and welcome you into My presence, so that you also may be where I am." (John 14:1-3)

When Thomas questioned Jesus, He said: "I am the way, and the truth and the life; No one comes to the Father except through me" (John 14:6). Every spring we celebrate Easter, Resurrection Sunday. When Steve and I were in the Middle East in 1972 we learned that the greeting of Christians on Easter is "He is risen," and the response back is, "He is risen indeed!"

The Apostle Paul reminds us in I Corinthians 15:3, "Christ died for our sins according to the scriptures. That he was buried and was raised to life again on the third day." The Resurrection is real.

Paul goes on to say that, after the Resurrection, Christ appeared to Peter, to the Twelve, to more than five hundred, to James, to the apostles, and then to himself. A friend of mine asked me if Jesus had been a real figure, a fact of history. Yes, yes, and yes.

The Scripture goes on to say that, if it were not for the resurrection, our faith would be in vain. I am so thankful for the resurrection life that He has given me through the Holy Spirit and, because of the resurrection of Jesus, I can look forward to meeting him face to face with my loved ones. As the song says, "I Can Only Imagine."

An excellent book, "*The Case for Christ*" (which has been made into a movie) will help answer your questions if you doubt. The author, Lee Strobel, an investigative reporter and a professed atheist, started the research for this book to disprove Christianity. The historical evidence he discovered was so overwhelming that he was convinced of the truth of the resurrection and became a follower of Jesus Christ.

Afterward

> Yet I am always with you, You hold me by my right hand. You guide me with your counsel, And afterward, you will take me into glory. (Psalm 73:23,24)

When I wondered in the depth of my grief if I could keep living, God impressed that word "*afterward*" on me *and it was life giving.*

My afterward has not come yet, and if you are reading this, neither has yours! Please embrace the Way, the Truth, and the Life *before*, so that in your *after*, you and I will meet again. Someday I will be welcomed into God's presence. My greatest prayer is that you will be a committed Jesus follower, experience his abundant life now, and then afterward I will see you there too.

I wrote the following song as my testimony:

May 5, 2009, by Judith King (The verses are based on Psalm 16). These are the words; the piano tune is still in my fingers.

His Love Endures Forever

Chorus
You are my life, there is no other,
Jesus, the Lover of my soul,
You're my Savior, my King, my Redeemer, forever
My love song from body, heart, and soul.

Verse 1
I will praise You Lord, You counsel me,
You guide me through the night.
It's your strong hand that holds me,
Your Presence gives me sight.

Verse 2

I have set the Lord before me,
He stands at my right hand,
I'll surely not be shaken,
In his presence firmly stand.

Verse3

My heart is glad my Jesus,
My body takes your rest.
You'll never, never leave me,
You're there through every test.

Verse 4

You have shown to me the path of life,
Your joy has been my gift,
At your right hand are pleasures,
With love, my head you lift.

Verse 5

So I dance with you into my life,
Forever, be your friend,
I'll walk with you and sing your praise,
Right up until the end.

Miracle of mercy through music

I was recounting to my friends recently how a *miracle* of *mercy* (and grace) and *music* coalesced for me. A year after Steve's death I was suffering with a very painful bone-on-bone knee joint. During the long night it was so bad I thought that I would have to call an ambulance and go to the hospital.

I got dressed and unlocked the front door for easy ambulance access and thought I would lie down on my bed one more time. I was desperate again, "*Jesus, please help me.*" Out of the blue, I heard my stereo in the other room start playing a song, one of my favorites: "Be strong and take courage, do not fear or be dismayed, for the Lord your God is with you and He will show you the way."

Who turned on the stereo? There was no one in the house, I was alone. And ... this song was in the middle of one of five CDs on a stack. I called out to see if my son had come over. Not. As I listened to the song, a peace came over me and I was freed from all pain.

Was there an angel in the house turning on my stereo? I don't think I'll go and see, I thought with some fear and trepidation. And I soon had fallen into a deep, peaceful, pain-free sleep.

A miracle of music and mercy?

I believe so.

Gloria Deus

Appendix

The Lillian and Russell John Briggs Family

Joyce Isabelle Wilson, age 79, lived in Toronto, Ontario and has four children and five grandchildren. She died in 2011.

William James Briggs, age 80, lived in Hamilton Ontario and has four children and twelve grandchildren. He died in 2015.

Russell Bruce Briggs, age 63, has six children and twelve grandchildren. He died in 2002.

Judith Evelyn King, (born January 1, 1944), lives in Grand Rapids, MI and has two children and seven grandchildren.

Barbara Joanne Green, age 65, lived in Newmarket, Ontario and has three children and five grandchildren. She died in 2013.

The Evelyn and James King Family

Gordon King, (born June 8, 1932) lives in Guelph, Ontario, has two children, six grandchildren, and 3 great-grandchildren.

Lynn White, (born May 20, 1940) lives in Toronto, Ontario, has four children and twelve grandchildren.

David Stephen King, age 63, (born April 2, 1942), lived in Grand Rapids, MI and has two children and seven grandchildren. He died on July 30, 2005.

About Judith E. King

Judith E. King, LMSW, ACSW, is a Christian mental health professional in Grand Rapids, Michigan. A native of Toronto, Ontario, Canada, she is a graduate of the University of Toronto and the Toronto Conservatory of Music. She received her MSW (Master of Social Work) degree from Western Michigan University in 1985.

King has a private clinical practice, where her interests include caring for professionals in ministry, women's issues, and substance abuse. She has conducted original published research related to the integration of sound psychological principles, spiritual concepts, and a biblical worldview, using among other tools of therapy, Dr. Neil Anderson's "Steps to Freedom in Christ."

In her ministry of teaching, counseling, and music, she has traveled globally, both with her late husband, Dr. Stephen King, M.D., and also more recently as the Lord leads her individually into many other open doors. She and Stephen co-founded Sonlife Associates, their private practice in Grand Rapids, MI.

King serves on the board of directors of FICM (Freedom in Christ Ministries) USA, FICMI (Freedom in Christ Ministries, International), and R.E.A.P. (Restoration of Education and Advanced Programs) in West Africa. She is a founding member of AACC (American Association of Christian Counselors) and a member of NASW (National Association of Social Workers).

Earlier in life King directed adult and children's choirs, organized and ran various choral and orchestral festivals, and for nine years was a board member for the Grand Rapids Symphony. Today she enjoys a wide variety of music, joyfully plays her grand piano frequently, occasionally picks up her very old and precious violin, and sings whenever an opportunity arises.

King loves Lake Michigan's water, how it feels when floating, splashing, and jumping in the waves, and how it reflects mid-afternoon diamonds, beckoning the upcoming glorious setting of the sun.

Happily she has a son and daughter-in-law, a daughter and son-in-law, and seven cherished grandchildren.